ON MASTERING AIKIDO

2nd EDITION

ON MASTERING AIKIDO

*Nine Dialogs on Principles -
From Black Belt to Master*

2ND EDITION

By
Daniel Linden

Foreword
By Mitsugi Saotome

Illustrations
By Olaf Schubert

ON MASTERING AIKIDO

By Daniel Linden

Basswood Press
Orlando, Florida
2nd Edition

ON MASTERING AIKIDO
*Nine Dialogs on Principles
From Black Belt to Master*
2ND EDITION

By Daniel Linden

Published by
Basswood Press
Orlando, Florida

All rights reserved. No part of this book may be reproduced or transmitted in any form or by any means, electronic or mechanical., including photocopying, recording, or by any information storage and retrieval system, without written permission from the publisher, except for the inclusion of brief quotations in a review.

All dialogs and other text by Daniel Linden
This is a work of fiction and no quotes may be attributed to any individual except the author.

Copyright © 2011 by Basswood Press

ISBN 1456562487

Second Edition

Library of Congress Control Number: 2004090408

The Dialogs

Table of Contents

- Acknowledgements 9
- Foreword 11
- Introduction 13

- *The Dialogs*

- Use the Force, Luke 19
- The Nexus and Break Points 43
- The Center 71
- Defining Aikido 89
- On Spirituality 111
- On Timing 131
- On Technique 151
- Triangulation in Aikido 167
- Strategy 189
- Afterword 215
- Glossary 217

For my wife Laurie, as always.

*And to Michael Dougher, R.I.P.
A warrior, and a true friend.*

Acknowledgements

Although most people who appear in this book exist, none of these conversations ever took place.

The dialogs in this book are the distillation of many conversations that have taken place over thirty-five years. Any inconsistency you might perceive concerning the things that are written and what you think you might know of the individuals quoted, is okay. People change often and what might be perceived as truth in one decade can be seen as myth or dogma in the next. At one time or another most of what transpires here happened and the things that I have reported that these individuals are alleged to have said…, well, they might actually have been said. Or not. Think of this as a work of instruction, not history.

Thanks to all my students, past and present. And, of course, special thanks to my lovely wife Laurie. Without her I probably couldn't find the dojo. In truth, without her I probably wouldn't have a dojo.

Preface to the Second Edition

Six years have passed since writing On Mastering Aikido. Time flies when you're having fun. Many of the people who appear in this work are no longer around. One, my dear friend Mike, died shortly after the first edition was published. I dedicate this second edition to his memory. Mike Dougher left us at age 46. He left behind his beautiful wife Shayla and three daughters. His last moments were spent on the Aikido mat doing a fine demonstration. May he rest in peace. His ashes are scattered at the Shoshin Aikido Dojo.

I am no longer a member of ASU. Mr. Saotome sent me a letter recently and I would like to quote a short excerpt or two. He states "...You are a master in your own right" and "I have nothing to teach and I wish you the best in your life..." I was thrilled to receive this.

I spent over thirty years as his student and am one of the rare individuals that he has so released from his tutelage. I wish him and all members of ASU the very best, as well. Now I have started a new organization called Modern American Martial Art Systems. I feel that aikido is a fine police art and literally 90% of what we do is still the traditional study of Aikido, but I now incorporate modern American boxing, karate and judo movements into the aikido training to make it more effective. Everything else that has changed since the first edition is in the text. Keep training hard!

Dan

Foreword

Aikido is not a simple martial art, but a profound study of dynamic communication to discover a secure society, a peaceful nation and a peaceful world. Since dynamic implies constant change and growth every Aikido instructor has a different approach and understanding of the principles underlying the art. In large part this understanding is determined by life experiences.

Dan Linden's life experiences as a warrior in Viet Nam and many years as a security expert for the City of Orlando, Florida have formed his Aikido. Warrior and protector of society, two sides of the same coin, are both necessary to O'Sensei's dream of the protection of all life and of our world. Dan's pursuit of the spiritual reality of Aikido has enriched, refined and deepened the understanding forged by his life experiences. He has been my close student for many years. I am proud of this student and of his unique and inspirational approach to Aikido.

Mitsugi Saotome

Mitsugi Saotome, Aikido Shihan
Thanksgiving Day, 11/27/2003

The Eight Pillars of Aikido Wisdom

Ki

Nexus

Center

Timing

Strategy

Technique

Break Points

Triangulation

The Dialogs

Introduction

Long, descriptive sentences bore me to tears. Reading Kant, Descartes, Joyce or James is torture. I love Plato however, and that dialog on phenomenology by George Berkley? It's just great stuff. Why? Plato and Berkley wrote in dialog form.

I am a reader who likes to skip ahead to the good parts. I'd wager most readers already feel the desire to jump ahead to the first chapter of this book and skip this introduction. I know I would. Give me dialog. I am addicted to quotation marks.

Those individuals who only look at the world through the eyes of art never see the mystery and complexity of the analytical mind. Those who only look at the world through the eyes of science never see the beauty. Aikido is a martial way, a *do,* which is almost wholly thought of as art. This book tries to see it analytically and define what it is that we actually do to achieve mastership.

My career in Aikido began back in 1971 at Northern Illinois University. I was going to school on the G. I. Bill and studying philosophy under Doctors Lester Embrey and G. Stormer, great guys who loved the classics and taught phenomenology. I discovered Aikido one cold, dreary night and it took all my powers of concentration to think of anything else from that time onward.

I've been very fortunate. Somehow, time and travel have allowed me to train under many of the truly great masters of this art. Names like Tohei, (both Akira and Koichi), Osawa, Yamaguchi, two Ueshibas, and Saotome are on that list Yet I can honestly say that until I allowed myself to explore the mysteries of Aikido without the constraints and imperfections of another mind constantly imposing and interfering I was not able to really actualize aikido as O'Sensei imagined.

Saotome was my last teacher. All the others were visiting professors that gave much and flavored the experience of learning Aikido. He was the pasta and potatoes and steak. He has been my daily bread and butter. But like all great chefs and gourmets one must leave the pedestrian back streets and small cafes and go out into the real world and explore and find the truth for oneself. In order to cook you must eat the world.

In Crescent City, Florida, back in 1976, I started my first dojo, then, in 1979 founded the Rocky Mountain Aikikai in Denver Colorado. Back in Florida, teaching Aikido to beginners at the University of Central Florida from 1985-1989 I realized that it was time to begin a serious school dedicated to mastering this art.

Shoshin Aikido Dojo is the result. Here we train instructors, have an international student body representing, Germany, Syria, Israel, Canada, Trinidad, Turkey, Ukraine, Puerto Rico, England, South Africa and other countries and focus on the essentials of mastering the art of Aikido.

My method of presenting the principles of mastership in this book is, I believe, unique. Although all master instructors I know teach the principles I know of none who use a similar approach. It has been a challenge and a pleasure to organize and systematize these principles and to display them in common English terms using the dialog form.

I applied the discipline of project management to this effort. Mind mapping, priority stacking and other techniques can cross disciplines and allow an easier approach toward understanding concepts that are very difficult to comprehend.

I have enjoyed using the dialog form. It should be understood that although the method allows easy comprehension, mere understanding is not enough to achieve mastership. To quote every teacher in my school..., "Train harder!" Each principle must be understood in context with the others and each must be practiced until it is understood in the deepest part of your soul.

The world of Aikido is changing. The art of peace originally founded by M. Ueshiba, (O'Sensei) was never meant to be static, never meant to be frozen in the mid twentieth century. It was meant to evolve. Aikido is as dynamic as the people who train and teach it.

With the publication of *The Harmony of Nature* Saotome presented the world with his view of O'Sensei's vision of Aikido. As his direct student I felt that I was privileged with a unique perspective and felt obligated by my commitment to him to present my own view. That it goes way beyond anything he dreamed is normal. It is the way of the world that student should move beyond his teacher. If not, the teacher is a failure. His top instructors have learned his ways and moved forward and beyond him and it is to his credit that he has not hindered this.

In *On Mastering Aikido*, I have taken my vision of the ascendant principles of mastership and interpreted them in my own unique American way. I have done something original in the mysterious Eastern world of the martial arts, interpreting the principles of Aikido into Western terminology and making them more accessible to the advanced student.

This is proper. This is the way it should be. As teachers and times age, students become teachers and grow into their roles. They interpret and discover new truths. They build bridges across gulfs of knowledge. They find new ways to discuss and teach old concepts; they find ways that enhance and make these concepts more beautiful and complete. There is a harmony to this evolution that is perfect in the nature of God and the universe. We grow old and die. Our children become the parents and then they become old. This is normal.

Wisdom is not knowledge; it is interpretation of information. So, in Aikido, the wisdom is in how we interpret the principles. I have broken the principles into eight categories: ki, technique, timing, break points, triangulation, strategy, center and nexus. Each concept is discussed in a dialog with students. I feel that I have offered a new perspective for all those who have struggled with these concepts for many years.

Are these perspectives different? Yes, certainly. Are they the best interpretation for some? Yes, again. Are they the only interpretation? No, of course, not. They are my interpretation. I have worked with students using my method and the results are simply wonderful. The way is very effective and should be studied and discussed by everyone. The method will not work for everyone, however. That is why we have so many teachers. Each brings his perspective and wisdom to the classroom and each gives us this wisdom in a different way.

The beauty of the written word is that everyone can read and study a teacher's system and decide for himself if that way is the right way for him. *On Mastering Aikido* is the most original work to come out for many long years. Too often people buck the system and disrupt the "norm" just for the sake of doing it. Until now, no one in the world of Aikido has ever done any thinking "outside the box". The time has come and the world of Aikido is ready. *On Mastering Aikido* is the result. It validates my teaching.

I have not attempted to teach Aikido in this book. That is for your Sensei. I have organized the principles that are required for mastering Aikido. By organizing and cataloging in English terms, I have attempted to make them more accessible and easier to incorporate into daily training.

It is well known that we train hard here at Shoshin Aikido Dojo, both in principles and in technique. We train from every conceivable attack. Using all of the standard Aikido attacks, boxing, karate, wrestling and anything else I can think of, we try to apply the principles to the techniques of defense. I have told students to go hit the heavy bag a thousand times a day for the next one hundred days because they needed to gain confidence and build strength. Students have been instructed to take a lawn chair and go sit and watch a daylily bloom. They needed to embrace patience.

Although this dojo is famous for the rigors of training, we have always been most focused on the principles and their application to self-defense technique. In short, the ferocious tenacity displayed here every day is the lifeblood of training for mastership. I hope these dialogs will inspire all those who read them to train fearlessly with open minds and hearts, and to understand and apply these principles to everything they embrace, both on the mat and off. Aikido is for real life. You can quote me.

Daniel Linden

Shoshin Kanji by Daniel Linden

The Dialogs

Chapter 1

Use the Force, Luke

Ki (life force, chi, prana) is the real mystery. *Ki* is the one intangible that we can't pin down with another definition, another explanation, and another description. *Ki* is. We have all, (most of us) read countless works on the Tao, or Dao, Zen, Spiritualism, Theosophy, Eastern works like the Upanishads, the Baghivad Gita, Books of the Dead, the Don Juan books, books, books, and more books. We have seen the Star Wars movies and heard all about The Force. We have trained to practice unbendable arm and that sitting and standing thing. But how many of us have actually experienced *ki*, or any force remotely resembling anything that is not explainable by any other means? Very few, if truth be told. But, and here is the caveat, there have definitely been a few. Once you experience it, you can never deny it. Darn it.

It would be much easier to say that *ki* is a nice idea and a good invention that keeps junior students training. They'd train until they realized that *ki* is only another word for the power generated by the fully integrated athlete. After much time, effort, and training, they'd see that it is only another word for knowing how the body works, but that it is in no way mystical or supernatural. But that isn't exactly true.

Ki energy is so tangible it can rock you to the depths of your body, soul and spirit. It can be a physical force that is understandable to even raw, untrained beginners. The obvious problem with merely going out and showing this truth is that there aren't even a handful of individuals who have ever been capable of manifesting this energy and most of the ones I have known are now dead. And they didn't honor me by leaving me the secret. Well, that isn't true. One did. One other tried. I'm just not smart enough, strong enough, or perhaps I'm merely unwilling to train my life away on what is at best, fun, and at worst merely a good parlor trick.

Ki is everywhere and in everything, but that being said – so what? Does a fish know about water? It does if it gets caught and thrown on shore, but otherwise? Water is just the medium in which it exists. Sometimes it might experience a shift in the medium – as in a current flow – but otherwise it just swims along, eating, making other little fish, and then dying. We are people, we exist, we move along making other little people, do a little dance, make a little love, etc… and then die. But once in a while we are made aware that the life force exists – remember that current thing – and for a moment we are conscious of it.

The blessing and curse of being human is magnified by our curiosity and our tendency to want to control and take advantage of everything around us. How did the Bible put it? Take dominion over? Well, we feel that current flow for an instant and we think, '…hey, I like that, I can control someone without even touching them...' And of course, then we want it. We want to use it. We want to control it.

But ki just is. It is the medium in which every living thing and every inanimate thing moves about. We can practice until the cows come home and never learn to be able to manipulate it. In that, George Lucas was rock on. He said, "The force is strong in that one," leaving one to assume that in all others it is merely there. The average schmuck on the street has about as much chance of becoming a Jedi Knight as, well, as you or me.

So what do we make of all this? There is a lot still to be said. My young Paduan, er, student, Luke came over to help me work on the pottery studio we are building at Shoshin Dojo. He has been the recipient of constant "Use the Force, Luke" comments his entire life. He shrugs and laughs it off, but there is a keen and abiding interest that has been spurred on for over twenty years.

Luke "Sensei, you often remark that ki is not something that can be taught, but how does anyone ever learn it unless someone teaches them?"

Linden "Luke I've only known two people who would manifest obvious ki. One was a medical doctor who had studied psychiatry and had practiced in South America where he studied a discipline known as Shamanism. The other was Osawa Sensei. They were both very old when we met – both in their eighties, but they were vigorous, strong and full of life. There are others who I am certain could, if so inspired, demonstrate obvious manifestations of ki, but choose (wisely, I believe) not to do so.

"The doctor, his name was Roxy Martin, wanted me to study with him, he said that I had the potential for something. I didn't get what at the time, but he said that it was something that he could teach me. He was getting to the point in life that he wanted to pass on his knowledge. Unfortunately I was suffering from a near terminal illness at the time, one common to those in their early twenties. I was dumb as a box of hammers and didn't understand what he wanted to tell me. Not all or even most of it, although the older I get the more of his teachings come back. Also I should mention the fact that I already knew everything there was to know about everything and most likely didn't have room for any more real knowledge.

"I was teaching Aikido, and thought I knew what ki was all about, too. I had started a small class in Crescent City, an old citrus town in North Central Florida. We met under the big oak trees in the park in the middle of town. I guess everyone who ever wanted to do Aikido has wanted to teach it, as if that is the culmination of achievement."

Luke "Not that I disagree, but why is that? Not everyone who studies karate or judo wants to teach it."

Linden "It is probably because we have no other markers of success. You can enter karate tournaments and win trophies and such, or actually get the thrill of winning in open combat. Heck, you can train for and go to the Olympics in Judo. In Aikido you just plod along, year after year until you either get asked to teach a class or go start your own dojo. We don't really have any other trophies - if you discount rank, and even judo and karate have rank. We don't win anything. We don't get to have these great catharses of emotion like winning a tournament or being beaten in the final round and then gritting our teeth and fighting back the next time. We just throw people and watch them take *ukemi*. We don't even get to throw them, really. They take *ukemi*. No wonder we wander off and start dojos…"

Luke "Okay, okay, I get it. Really. I've never really understood the manifestation of ki in training, other than unbendable arm. Can you explain how a master or at least really senior practitioners express what they are doing in terms of ki?"

Linden "I can only speak for myself. When I am attacked I rely on my intuitive ability to guide me into either a fore or aft position, or *irimi/tenkan*. That intuitive ability has been sharpened on the whetstone of ki training. I allow myself to feel, first. My next application of ki is during the establishment of the nexus, or what we have traditionally called joining. Here I only allow as much contact as necessary. I do not want *uke* to feel threatened by this. Once the nexus is established I move my hips so that they are directly facing the nexus and begin to draw out *uke's* center. Extending ki in such a way as to allow me to be aware of his center and balance does all of these things.

"Next I make whatever physical contact is necessary with *uke* flow through my body. I do this by closing the gap beneath my arms and keeping the nexus directly in my center. I lift energy from the earth by being in contact with it, raise it up through my legs into my body and extend it towards uke's break point. I lead the nexus away from uke's center toward that same break point until he is compromised and uke takes *ukemi*.

"All during this process I maintain a relaxed state with muscle tension mostly focused on keeping my center and the nexus aligned and keeping the nexus in my center as I move. This is what most people call 'extending ki'. What it is, really, is completely experiencing your connection to the earth and maintaining awareness of your connection with the earth and with the *uke*. During this process uke usually gets extended or drawn out of his center. I stay relaxed and in contact with *uke*, experience his extension, and find it easy to know when he has reached a breaking point.

"That idea we call unbendable arm – it is really quite a misnomer – is taught to introduce beginners to the notion that relaxed strength is greater than rigid strength, but is usually done with a fixed arm position. I don't think in twenty-five years of teaching I have ever seen anyone teach it while having the individual flex his arm. And yet that is how we actually use it. When we join and move we are joining with that same unbendable arm, or extended arm, if you will. When we move, collapse, rotate, pronate, supinate, or extend we must maintain that same extension and connection. Yet no one ever seems to train the basic form with motion. We do this on an active basis, you know.

"It is the conscious understanding and awareness of these processes that I like to call ki training."

Luke "Do you think people are really fixated on learning about ki? Is this something that most people who do Aikido believe in?"

Linden "I think it is something that most people believe in whether they do Aikido or not. I'll tell you a story.

"There was a teacher, I guess he should remain nameless to protect the guilty, who decided to demonstrate ki at a party one night. What he did was this... he asked for a banana from a bowl and then tapped it with a chopstick. Those people watching him were then asked to peel the banana, and lo and behold, where he had touched the fruit, it was sliced as clean as a scalpel. Everyone was amazed and he then asked for another banana and this time he tapped the fruit with the chopstick twice and offered it for inspection.

"They peeled this one and it too was cut cleanly twice. Everyone was absolutely amazed. They broke out more chopsticks and handed out bananas and then proceeded to whack those poor bananas into mush trying to get one to slice or even break. Someone ran out to the store for more bunches and this went on for some time. Now if truth were ever to enter into this story it is a fact that some very high-ranking individuals were a party to this banana battering, but they too, will remain unmentioned. Most were low level *yudansha* at the time."

Luke "Are you going to tell me how he did it? How he cut the banana with just ki energy?"

Linden "Excuse me?"

Luke "Are you going to tell me how ki can cut through fruit without hurting the peel?"

Linden "Well, it can't, Luke. Haven't you been listening?"

Luke "Okay. How did the fruit become separated from itself inside the skin if you can't cut it with ki?"

Linden "See this is what I'm talking about. People assume that ki is real and can be manipulated. This is like what a magician does. Everyone sees him float a woman above the ground and then wave a wand over and under her. Maybe he'll even pass a hula-hoop over her and nothing seems to be holding her up but his magic energy. People love this, but it's all a hoax, all smoke and mirrors. But people want to believe."

Luke "Sensei, are you going to tell me how the fruit got cut?"

Linden "Sure. Before the party he took a banana from the bowl and pushed a sewing needle into a crease, you know, a seam – on the banana. He wiggled the needle back and forth and then pulled it out. He did the same to the second banana. Then he carefully arranged them in the bowl so that the first one to the hand would be the one with only one cut. Simple"

Luke "That's ridiculous. Why would he do something like that?"

Linden "I don't know, for fun, maybe? All I know is that twenty years later I'm still telling the story. Sometimes people take too many things too seriously and a good laugh puts things back into perspective. Like telling you about my early days and Crescent City, I'm trying to put things into perspective."

Luke "Right. You were telling about the old guy in your shop. That doctor."

Linden "Exactly, it happened back when I was your age. See, Doctor Martin had lived in Crescent City until his wife passed away. He closed up the family home and practiced in New York for a few years and then came back to Crescent City, which is when I made his acquaintance. He had been a part owner in a large citrus concern and he decided to close that as well as sell the house. He walked into my shop one day and requested that all the locks be changed on the house, business and a couple other properties he had. I made the arrangements and as we talked we started to wander off subject.

"I kept getting the feeling he was trying to tell me something without coming right out and saying the words. It was like he would use a word and then wait to see if I had any idea what he had referred to."

Luke "Give me an example. Can you remember anything specific?"

Linden "I don't know. He was talking about his back hurting, he had been moving paver blocks and they weighed about sixty pounds apiece. Remember he was in his eighties. But he said that his back hurt and then said something like, 'Oh, I guess it could just be an unbalanced chakra.' I knew he was referring to the ascending and descending levels in the body that the yogis refer to. The energy centers, or focus points, whatever. But the thing is, I don't believe that anyone in Crescent City at that time would have had a clue what he was talking about and I think he was just trying to get a feel for what knowledge I had, for the things I had studied. Then he said something about me being young and wasting my time on Buddhism, and this freaked me seriously because I was studying Buddhism intently in my spare time. And believe me, in Crescent City, Florida, you have a lot of free time.

"So I was a little offended at this and then the weird thing happened. He leaned over the counter about half way, you know, so his elbows were resting on it, and then he said, 'I didn't say Buddhism, I said boozing.' And then I couldn't breathe.

"I don't mean I was in shock. I mean I couldn't breathe. It was like something was pushing on my chest and not letting it rise up and take in any air. I actually looked down at my chest and when I looked up he was smiling at me. And then I could breathe. It didn't last three seconds. He turned around and said he would expect me at his house the next day in the afternoon and that we would go to the citrus grove after I was done with the house. Then he left."

Luke "Did you feel like you had been challenged? Like he was dangerous?"

Linden "No, not at all. Actually it was a lot like being in the presence of a great spiritual leader. I met a Rabbi once like that and I knew a teacher named Harry McKinght who had that effect. You could feel his innate goodness and kindness as soon as he walked in the door. But you are also aware of his power and authority as well. Doc Martin was like that. That was not the only time he showed me his power. I spent a great deal of time with him over a few months and we spoke constantly of the study of higher power, ki, shamanism, Buddhism, astral travel – something in which he claimed to be a master and many other things.

"By the next afternoon we dropped any façade that there was not a serious student and teacher event happening. I sought knowledge and he talked and showed me things. He was very old and had enormous knowledge of a vast number of things. He had been everywhere and done most everything. And I believe he knew he would die soon. His family was a terrible disappointment to him. His sons and daughter, grandchildren and great grandchildren did not have any interest in the things that he did. They were just ordinary folks and lived their lives in ordinary ways, but Roxy Martin, man, the force was strong in that one."

Luke "Okay, when you say something like that I don't know if you've been putting me on or not."

Linden "Luke, do you imagine for one minute that George Lucas made all that up? The business with the Force and the Jedi Knights is as old as humanity. Think of it as a genetic memory of when we were closer to the earth and the event we call nature. When people say ki, or the Force we know intrinsically what they are referring to, because we have that human memory of these things. Every primitive people we have ever studied had someone in the tribe who could commune with the spirit world. For these people it is as real as the dirt beneath their feet.

"You no more have to define beauty or love than you do ki, chi, prana, or any of a number of expressions that mean life force. Remember, a fish has no word for water.

"Doc Martin had a powerful ki force. I had only been doing Aikido for about five years then, but even as dumb and inexperienced as I was I could recognize that an amazing master was there in front of me. He didn't look like an old yogi, or have any of the attributes that we think of when we say spiritual master, yet he was an accomplished master. I think Osawa Sensei would have recognized him immediately. But he did not shine for everyone. For most people he was just old Doc Martin. He was irascible, ornery, and cantankerous, drank too much, was short tempered and rude. But most of those things might just have been because he only had a few months to live. Or it could have been that he was simply that way. People make way too much of this nonsense that Masters are nice and lovable. Mostly they aren't. They just don't have time or patience with people's nonsense."

Luke "Well, what other things did he do to show you that he could manipulate ki? Can you be specific?"

Linden "You know, Luke, in the context of this discussion I don't believe I want to discuss Doc Martin any more. Maybe we'll come back to him and his teachings another time, but as I talk about him now I don't feel all that comfortable. Not like I thought I would. The things he showed me and taught me were, well, they were for me. I think for now it suffices that he existed and did control ki and he showed me his abilities. Like I said, once you experience it, you can never deny it. Darn it."

Luke "Okay, what about Osawa, Sensei? Can you talk about him?"

Linden "Sure. I've told that story often enough, it's no secret. But haven't you tried to learn to extend ki yourself? What have you done to attempt to access this form of energy? What strides have you made? Any success at all? I know your Mom is interested in these things and studies yoga and military arts with an attention to power."

Luke "I don't think I've accomplished anything at all. There are times when I feel like I've done something really well, but nothing that makes me feel as if I have tapped an extra power source. Sometimes when I was playing baseball I would have a moment when a swing connected just right or when it seemed as if I were an instrument of some other power, like when a ball would break and I wasn't expecting it, but the bat would be in motion and hit it out to the fence. But then

I might have just gotten lucky with a really good swing."

Linden "Well, they say that hitting a round ball flying toward you at ninety-five miles an hour with a round bat is the most difficult athletic feat that there is."

Luke "Not to mention the sixty thousand people who are yelling at you and screaming for you to die, if you're in an opposing park. Can you imagine a golfer, who, by the way, hits a ball carefully placed on a little wooden tee that isn't moving, have the entire gallery screaming at him while he lines up a shot? What a bunch of wimps."

Linden "You don't have to put other sports down just because you played baseball. I agree with you, by the way. Golf isn't a sport. It's a game. On the other hand could you imagine if the baseball player had to hit the ball through a hole the size of a dinner plate to score? It would make that golfer seem like a hero, wouldn't it?"

Luke "Okay, don't get me started. Still, sometimes you would wonder how a certain hit happened; it would be so different, so powerful. So I don't know if maybe I was using ki at those times or if I just held the bat a little different."

Linden "I don't know anything about baseball, but it strikes me that it is a pretty good medium for consciously extending ki energy with the swinging of the bat and the throwing of the balls. Anytime you practice those kinds of movements you can certainly tap a little more power by consciously trying to extend the level of power through and out. That is why we always keep our hands open while practicing technique. It is easier to extend ki if we let it flow through our finger tips."

Luke "But Sensei, you always keep closed fists. At least most of the time."

Linden "That is my training, now. I am practicing extending ki through my knuckles and closed fist. I practice extending ki through my elbows, knees, feet, forehead, and anywhere else I might use as a striking surface. That is my training, not yours. You should literally do as I say, here, not as I do.

"As we go through the different stages of our training we focus on different things. This is natural and normal. You are still trying to stay upright and get through the rudimentary forms of technique with your hands open. A *shodan* will be using a constant breathing and moving to generate ki strength. A *sandan* should have internalized the breathing movement exercises and start to extend ki into his technique and by *godan* or *rokudan* you should be able to extend ki into and through every part of the body, both yours and your opponent's."

Luke "I'm confused. I thought you said that you have only experienced ki a couple times in your life. Now I hear you talk about ki being extended everywhere all over the mat."

Linden "Do you feel great ki energy when you work with me? Don't blow smoke at me, tell me what you feel and think."

Luke "You are unbelievably strong. I can't imagine how you produce so much power when you throw me. But, I don't feel that it isn't something that you couldn't learn to do physically after thirty-five years of training. I mean, I know athletes that can hit a ball out of the park each time they swing the bat. Each time, but they have great technique and they are really strong. You are the same. You're the smoothest person I've ever seen on his feet and you're a big man, but I don't feel any extraordinary power coming off your fingertips."

Linden "Good. I don't either. But I believe that there is some level of it there, nonetheless. How much? Who knows? Who knows how much of my power is ki and how much is ten thousand hours of training? But I know this, if I don't train for its eventuality, I will never have it at my disposal. I believe I lost the chance for gaining it the easy way."

Luke "Just a minute, please. You have to back up on a couple things. Ten thousand hours of training? The easy way? I want to make sure I understand what you are talking about."

Linden "Five hours a week for thirty-three years plus seminars and times when I was more enthusiastic than I am now. About ten thousand hours of training, give or take. Okay? And as far as the easy way, what I was referring to then was Doctor Martin.

"Back before I left Crescent City I was talking to Doc Martin about Aikido all the time. You know how you are when you get really interested in something and you are young. Older people have more of an ability to mitigate interests, but the young become obsessed and spend all their time focused on one thing. Well, I was young then, no doubt. One night we were having dinner at one of the fish camps down along the St. Johns River. I don't know if you know the kind of place I mean or not. Basically it's fried food, catfish, or meatloaf and mashed potatoes and gravy. Down home cooking, they call it.

"We had eaten and were driving back to Crescent City and I was on a roll about the martial arts and Aikido in particular when Doctor Martin asked me if I really wanted to become a master of fighting. He didn't say martial arts. He specifically asked if I wanted to be a master of fighting. I said I did, thinking that he was using his own term for martial arts and at the time believing that they were one and the same.

"When we arrived at his house we went into the main room. We had spent the last month clearing it out and disposing of the furniture and books and what not. For some reason, he had these red bricks that he didn't want left outside, so he had me bring them in and make a kind of big oblong square out of them right in the middle of the living room floor. This had taken me a week or so. The square was about eight feet long and about four or five feet wide. It was a lot of bricks. I couldn't begin to tell you why he was so concerned about them, but he just had to have them inside where they couldn't be stolen. Remember he was old.

"He asked me to lie down on the bricks and put my hands to my side. I did as I was asked with a certain trepidation. Truthfully, Luke I am not a very trusting individual. If you have ever seen Bruce Lee's **Enter the Dragon** you might remember the scene where the bad guy asks if the one fighter would put his head in a guillotine, then places the cat there. I don't remember the actor's name, but he says 'There are some things, beyond which, I will not do.' Then he reaches down and takes the cat out of the mouth of the guillotine. I am like that. My wife could ask me to put my head in something like that and I would refuse.

"I laid on those bricks for a minute or two until Doctor Martin came back. He sat down on a kitchen chair beside me. In his hands he held a knife, a wicked looking thing with a strange long handle. He said that he was going to show me something that would make me able to defeat anyone in fighting. He started to place the knife on my chest with the point towards my throat and the cutting edge straight up. I pushed his hand away and moved over away from him.

"He laughed and said not to be nervous and looked at me. I felt the same inability to breathe that I had experienced in the shop that first day. This time, however I was frightened. I don't know why. I slowly found my breath and moved over to where he was waiting. He slowly laid the knife on my chest again and began to talk to me, but I wasn't thinking about what he had to say. I could feel his presence everywhere and it just scared the living daylights right out of me. I pushed his hand off and rolled over. This time he let me go. I got up and laughed and asked him to just show me what he was going to do, but he shook his head and took the long knife away into the other room. I never saw it again.

"I have regretted that decision to run away from power for almost thirty years. In retrospect I know he would never have hurt me. In fact he was ready to give me a gift of power. What form it would have taken I am not sure, but I believe it would have been the gift of ki. I believe he was going to show me how to manifest ki toward the disposal of a threat. And I blew it. I ran away."

Luke "I don't believe it."

Linden "Oh, you can believe it all right. He was the same to me after as before, as if nothing had ever happened, but I was never the same. I felt like I had disappointed him or let him down, but it was never brought up. The next time I came back to Crescent City I had made my mind up to visit him and ask him again to show me what it was he had intended that night, but by then he had passed away. Actually regret is too simple and soft a word for what I feel. On the other hand he might have just been a crazy old man who wanted to scare me into training in Aikido for the next thirty years. And succeeded."

Luke "What about Osawa Sensei?"

Linden "That was different. Osawa Sensei was touring with Yamaguchi Sensei on the occasion of the tenth anniversary of the Founder's death. He had with him a disciple of the Reverend Deguchi from the Omoto religious sect and the classes were very spiritually oriented. We did lots of breathing exercises, we exercised the *kotodama* and did many techniques to help build the center and develop ki."

Luke "How old were you at this time?"

Linden "I was twenty-seven or twenty-eight. Sensei had only recently been to Denver for a vacation and a seminar in my dojo, The Rocky Mountain Aikikai. Osawa Sensei came in the spring and someone found a large upstairs room in Boulder to hold his seminar in, an unlikely sort of location. I think they must have been going from place to place and training where they could – a very impromptu tour."

Luke "What was your rank then?"

Linden "I was a nidan then, full of myself and thought I knew everything. God, youth is so humiliating in retrospect..."

Luke "Why? Weren't you any good?"

Linden "You know you can push that New York thing just so far, young one. I was just fine, thank you. Probably exactly at *nidan*, maybe better... I had gone back to Sarasota for a winter camp and while there had invited a teacher to Denver. He came for the seminar and shortly after he returned home he called me to let me know that I had been raised up. He didn't need to do that. He could have asked me to come to a summer camp or hold another seminar and bring him back to Denver, but he didn't."

Luke "What was Osawa Sensei like?"

Linden "He was a small man, at least to me. And unlike Yamaguchi Sensei he didn't have a particularly hard or strong musculature. He seemed quite ordinary unless you were acting as his *uke*. I was quite fortunate that he used me a great deal. He was soft I guess you could say. Powerful, yet gentle. No, that's not quite right. He didn't seem to have any hard edges. More of a magician than a hard line martial artist, but I guess that could have been his age. He moved with a great deal of spiritual energy, completely in his center. He was really a beautiful old man."

Luke "How did he demonstrate his ki to you? Was it just in the way he moved or threw you? I know you've said that Koichi Tohei was the strongest person who had ever thrown you. How was that different from Osawa Sensei?"

Linden "Koichi Tohei was, or may still be, I don't know, an almost inhuman force. He could toss you twenty feet if he wanted to bother. He was just unbelievably strong, and don't forget he was a big man as well, for a Japanese. Handsome and very dignified when I saw him, he was very impressive. Osawa Sensei, on the other hand, was not impressive at all. He was small and old, but you could tell he was a kind man and that his heart was very gentle. Maybe I'm wrong, but that was my impression of him. They were completely different. They were as different as Erik Guzman Sensei and me. Really polar opposites, yet both amazing in what they were able to do.

"The ki demonstration came out of the clear blue sky. It was totally unexpected. Osawa Sensei called me up to be his uke. I attacked with a *katatedori ryote mochi,* two hands attacking one wrist. He threw me in forward extensions a couple times and then took me down in a fairly powerful *iriminage.* As he finished his throw he leaned over me and held his hand about eighteen inches above my chest. With his other hand he motioned for me to rise. I leaned forward to push my way up but felt a powerful resistance. I realized that he was standing on my *gi.* I believed that his foot was on the part of my *gi* just under my arm because I couldn't push myself up. I looked down expecting to see his foot there but I was surprised to see both of his feet well away from me. He still stood there over me with a smile on his face motioning for me to get up and the harder I pushed the firmer I was held.

"It was like lightening striking. I suddenly realized what was happening to me – what he was doing. I believe in that instant I went into shock a little bit. He moved away and released me. I stood up and I admit I was a bit shaky from what had happened. He had to have understood my amazement because he motioned for me to go to the side of the mat where everyone else was sitting and watching.

"As I sat down, the guy I had traveled to the seminar with looked over at me. He was a powerful man, a former company commander in Viet Nam, an ex-Green Beret, and at the time he was President of the American Conference of Christians and Jews. A stand-up guy. He looked me in the eye with sizzling intensity and fairly spit out the words, 'That's bull----! No one can do that!' I can't imagine that Osawa Sensei knew what he had said, but when Ron turned his head back, Sensei was beckoning to him to come out and be his uke. He then threw Ron the exact same way and pinned him in the exact same way only this time I got to see how it was done."

Luke "How did he do it?"

Linden "I just told you. He pinned us both by holding his hand above us and willing us to stay on the ground and not get up. He just held his hand over us."

Luke "What did it feel like?"

Linden "Like he was standing on my *gi*. Like a pressure, kind of nebulous, but the more you fought it the more you realized its inexorable power. I can't describe it more than that. I've always wanted to ask Ron what he felt, but I never got the chance. When Osawa Sensei released him he walked off the mat and straight over to where his gym bag was against the wall, and walked out the door. I never saw him again. This was a man who had been hit. You remember that story, right?"

Luke "I don't know what you're referring to."

Linden "It's an old boxer's expression. Everyone has a belief in his own strengths and a belief in his opponent's weaknesses. So he makes a game plan by which to live, and fight. The expression goes, 'Everyone has a plan until he gets hit'. Well, Ron thought he had Aikido completely figured out. He thought he knew what the truth was. Then Osawa Sensei showed him that he didn't have a clue."

Luke "He got hit."

Linden "You bet."

Luke "But you did, too."

Linden "I was too young and stupid to think that what had just happened to me couldn't possibly happen. In fact, I'd been waiting for years for it to happen. For me, it just confirmed all my beliefs. How was I to know that Osawa Sensei was a Jedi Knight and the rest of us were farmers and bartenders?"

Luke "What about Seagal Sensei? Can he manipulate ki like that?"

Linden "Luke, I believe that those rare individuals who can do this share their gift sparingly. Lord only knows why Osawa Sensei gave this to me. I don't. I've spoken with people who studied with him in Hombu Dojo for years and they said that they had never seen him do anything like that. Even to the point that they implied I was lying about this."

Luke "What did you do about that?"

Linden "What can you do? Half the people in Aikido pray for something like that to happen to them. Most of the people I know would deny that it is possible at all. Just shrug your shoulders and go on and know that it actually happened to you. Not once, not twice, but a number of times."

Luke "With your Sensei?"

Linden "Boy, you just don't quit. Do you?"

Luke "Have you ever been to New York?"

Linden "Okay. No, not with him. I don't think he is strong that way. He is very quick and has great balance and timing, but he isn't any different than the rest of us. His level of ki is much the same as most sixth dans or so. Remember, he is a very small man. If he has the gift that Osawa had, he has never demonstrated it to anyone that I know of and I was his most personal and favorite student for years. But who knows? Curtis never played the guitar in front of me even though he is very good and I knew him for ten years. It is actually hard to say who might have it.

Luke "But why wouldn't he teach you this if it's important?"

Linden "Son, haven't you been listening? I've already been shown. I've been given great gifts, but I am not one who is able to reciprocate. I just don't have the juice. A little, oh sure, and maybe as I age I might be able to do a few parlor tricks. But it isn't important. It is only important to understand that it does exist and that if you train hard you can tap into a tiny bit of it. My students know exactly how complete my belief is and also know that I would be wasting my efforts to teach them more. Let me save that for…"

Luke "The force is strong in that one…"

Linden "Yeah! Do you get this yet? We are talking about the difference between knowing that Jesus Christ was a myth, a put up job, or the Son of God! We are talking about the difference between knowing that we landed on the moon or it was all done on a sound stage in Burbank. We're talking about the difference between knowing that ki is the vital life force of the universe or the mere suspicion or hope that it is. Luke, I know. It isn't some nebulous suspicion with me. I know. And because I have experienced it the way that I have, I can smell it when it is around me. Maybe not taste it, not be able to cook it or throw it out the window...but Son, I know when it is there. And I will tell you one more secret, one small one just for you. Ki is everywhere, in everything, and as thick and rich as my beef stew. But it isn't meant to be eaten.

"And that is really all I have to say about ki at this time."

Ki
By O'Sensei

The Dialogs

Chapter 2

The Nexus

When I watched Saotome Sensei move during that Cherry Blossom seminar in 2003, I could only see from the waist up. There were at least two hundred people on the mat. We were five or six rows deep just to bow in. Since I am tall and long at the waist I have always been able to see over most people during training and have, as a consequence, taken to sitting in the back rows. People can't see over or around me.

The interesting thing about training with most master Aikido instructors is that they do not ever tell you what you need to know to really understand what they are teaching. I am not certain if some of them even know what they are doing. I know several guitar players who are magnificent natural players but cannot present a specific chord if asked because they simply are not educated musicians. Mastership in Aikido is a physical thing, not an intellectual one, and there is the problem. Some teachers talk at length of stealing technique from O'Sensei. I have read accounts of students trying to gain insight and understanding of the forms used by other masters and having to be extremely furtive when taking notes or trying to gain exact knowledge of the particulars.

I don't believe most master instructors are really trying to keep the information from us. They might, in fact, be trying desperately for us to gain this knowledge. In truth, most really don't care if we master a particular technique that they are teaching. Their purpose is much higher. They want us to understand the principle behind the technique and this explains why they sometimes move from technique to technique so fast that often both partners don't get an equal chance to practice it. They simply are not concerned with the techniques. They are trying to get us to see the underlying archetypal form – the principle. It is difficult. Understanding comes slowly and through intense work. I believe that understanding is equal to the effort. However, I also believe that a few explanations of the particular relationships that are so evident to them and so elusive for most everyone else are very beneficial. These opinions are the distilled result of many years of observation of some great masters and as such are truly personal. They do contain great truths, however.

We were having dinner after class. Two senior instructors were with me, Terry and Ron. Terry has over twenty years Aikido experience and Ron over fifteen. We were waiting to place our drink order when Terry asked this question.

Terry "Linden Sensei, you have been mentioning a great understanding that came to you at Cherry Blossom Festival this year. Are you planning to share it or are you going to make us steal it from you?"

Linden "I already have."

Terry "Excuse me? Did I miss a class or something?"

Ron "Yeah, what is this?"

Linden " I have been teaching it since I got back. Every class contains everything I learned, the whole ball of wax. You haven't seen it?"

Terry " I think you have been moving beautifully and..."

Linden "I don't need to hear that stuff. Did you see the connection between *uke* and *nage* change after I returned?"

Terry "I've seen something. I am not sure what it is, though. You seem to be more connected to *uke*. You seem to be able to move through his power more effortlessly. Let's face it, you always could, though."

Ron "You seem to be more sure of the point where *uke* loses his balance and is moved to a place where he can no longer sustain the attack. You are moving to it without having to look for it or feel it. I'm talking micro-seconds, but I think I have noticed it."

Linden "And you would be correct, Ron. That is it exactly."

The waiter came by and asked what we wanted to drink. He told us the daily specials and what was not available. We ordered and then looked at the menus for a moment. I have come to really enjoy the no-smoking law for restaurants that went into effect in Florida this year. It had gotten to the point where I did not enjoy going out to eat at all because of all the second hand smoke I was forced to breathe. My wife and I would come home from going out to eat and have to change clothes on the back porch because we did not want our closet to smell of smoke for days afterward. I ordered a fish sandwich and turned back to Ron.

Linden "The point where *uke* and *nage* meet, is a nexus of energies that is continually changing. Each variation in attitude, and by that I mean Miyamoto Musashi's definition of attitude, each variation in speed, direction, power, and intensity changes the dynamic. Therefore, we need to be constantly correcting to accommodate these changes. These corrections are done by shifting the hips to move the nexus into the center, by moving the feet to triangulate the best path towards *uke's* break point, with timing, technique, and extending ki.

"Let me tell you a story. This happened years ago while I was living in Detroit. My boss sent me to install a complete security system, locks, alarms, the whole works in a house in one of the suburbs. The name on the ticket said Hearns. I got there and wow, talk about culture shock, everybody there looked like they were from the black mafia. I mean black silk suits, bowler hats, everybody in sunglasses, even inside the house – major black power trip. I'm working on the installation and after a while this very skinny dude comes over and starts to talk to me, find out what I'm doing. He's the only one dressed casual, chinos and a t-shirt, sandals. We talk and I tell him about the system I'm installing. One thing leads to another and we start to talk about Aikido.

"Now understand, I'm being polite, maybe even a bit condescending. This guy is not the brightest candle on the cake, but he's being nice to me, so I tell him the idea about ki energy and the way we move in Aikido.

Remember that I am only twenty-nine years old, had only been doing Aikido then for about ten or eleven years, but I thought I was really knowledgeable, and was trying to start a *dojo* in Detroit.

"After a while this guy drifts off and I finish the job. It was big, a big price tag. I'd done well. I'm about to leave and this bowler hat guy comes up and says 'Tommy wants you to come see him work out. You say something to him?' I respond, 'Tommy who?' He says, 'Tommy Hearns! Who you think you talking to?'

"Tommy Hearns. The Hit-Man. Tommy 'Hit Man' Hearns. Like the best middleweight fighter in the world. Who knew? He was little, maybe five eleven and skinny. I simply didn't realize whom I had been talking with. Anyway, the bowler hat guy gives me a card signed by Hearns that says to let me in anytime at this downtown address that turns out to be a gym.

"I go down a few weeks later and give the doorman the card and he leaves me out in the snow for about a half hour and then lets me in. Everybody stares at me until Hearns sees me, waves and nods. I guess I was suddenly cool because then everybody ignored me. I walked to the practice ring and leaned against the ropes and watched the coaches work with him and this other guy for a while – coaching moves, strategy, whatever. Finally everybody leaves the ring except the two fighters.

"Now this is what I am trying to get you to understand. When these two fighters faced off, the ki flow was so dense I almost got sick. I saw up close and personal what you don't see on television. I saw what people pay five thousand dollars for when they buy ringside seats. Tommy's right calf muscle twitched.

The other fighter's shoulder muscle rolled. Tommy's head jigged to the left. The opponent's stomach muscles twitched. The ki flow was so thick it was almost palpable. These fighters hadn't even thrown a punch yet but they were battling at a level you just cannot imagine.

"Every variation in direction, speed, attitude, angle, intensity, and power was not only being noted, it was being accounted for, analyzed, reacted to, anticipated and dealt with. This is before the battle was even met. It was the most devastating demonstration of the nexus I've ever witnessed. Yet neither of these combatants had any idea about what Aikido is, and could probably have cared less for an explanation. This is the thing. They were world-class athletes. The best of the best of the best, distilled from hundreds of thousands of individuals who endeavored to be where they were. There is a reason that those guys climb into the ring and battle as they do. They are better. They were both masters of so much that we endeavor to learn, without knowing for an instant that they knew it. They both understood the connection, the nexus so clearly. They were masters of ki extension. Just wild."

Ron "So you are saying that the nexus is the reaction between two people caught up in combat?"

Linden "No, it is the point where they meet. I think of the nexus as a connection that takes place between combatants. It is done in the hands, wrists, arms, shoulders – wherever you connect to lead the uke to his point of imbalance."

Ron "Even the feet?"

Linden "Why not? But it must be where we are in control. Where we are timed to complete the move.

Timing is the connection that takes place mentally – when you intrinsically understand that you are facing attack and realize that you need to find an opening to blend with the attack. The nexus is the actual connection that happens when your hands and wrists and forearms join in contact with the attack. They connect with the attacker at any of a thousand places as the attack happens. Wherever you make this contact – that is the nexus - and it must be maintained. If it is a push-hand, a deflection, or if the attacker has grabbed us – then it's easy to maintain the connection. So when you move the nexus into your center by shifting your hips, and you triangulate your stance by adjusting your feet - you eventually learn to control the encounter with your whole body, not your arms and hands. But the nexus must be maintained to sustain control."

Terry "It's like an intersection of forces, a place where all the highways of energy come together. And it keeps moving."

Linden "That's it. You have the idea. Now for years I have been aware of the importance of this intersection. I have learned that if you keep this intersection, this nexus, in front of you within a fairly well defined location, that you are able to move anyone with a minimum of force. That is basic. It's the idea that we always refer to when we say our 'center'. This is physical and isn't particularly interesting unless you are one of those individuals who like to wave your arms around and flail away far from your center. We must, as we move around, keep the nexus in our direct middle, a space only five or six inches wide directly in front of us. We achieve this by shifting the hips, keeping the action directly in front."

Terry "Like two inches below the navel, right?"

Linden "No. That refers to something else. The height doesn't matter, only that we maintain the nexus in the center. We move high or low, drop our center, bend our knees, even raise our arms high like in a sword swing as long as it stays in our center."

Terry "But why?"

Linden "I'm getting to that. Not the basic reason, but the real reason. Now, we know that the nexus must be maintained in our center and for years I understood that. What happened along the way was that I came to understand that one of the things that we do when we break an *uke's* balance is to take the nexus out of his center. We don't allow him to maintain his center. Basic, right? We're talking *kyu* rank stuff here.

"Now we also know that being human, we only, most of us, have two feet. We also have round heels. This makes for a perfect formula for imbalance, except that we are not only not imbalanced, but we have amazing balance. We are truly astonishing creatures because we understand perfectly how to accommodate our postures and position to maintain balance. It is really pretty hard to knock someone down or to push someone over. In fact, think about the game of football. The whole idea of the game, besides getting the most points, is to try and knock the ball carrier to the ground. And it is hard! You have three-hundred-pound defensive guys slamming into runners and grabbing them with both hands. Look, even the rules are made to make it easier on the defensive player – the runner can't use his hands except to push away with a stiff arm. So this runner is being chased by half a dozen guys who can grab him and slam into him and despite this he manages to run all over the field and score touchdowns without being taken down.

"Really guys, human beings are pretty hard to knock down if they don't want to go."

Ron Laughing. "I never thought of it that way."

Linden "Well, I've worked out with a couple of professional football players and they are pretty amazing. Like the boxers, they are distilled from the best of the best of the best. Anyway, you have these two feet with the round heels. If you push against someone's chest they tend to squat a bit to keep from falling over. They do this by keeping their shoulders directly over their feet and extending their butt backward while bending at the knees. This assumes that their feet are not in a foot-forward position, but side by side. Now when they squat a bit they are creating a third post that forms a kind of triangle, the strongest structure known. This triangle is directly opposite the direction of the push and straight down through the spine, out to the floor. That point should be apparent to anyone looking at the posture of the two individuals standing and pushing.

"If the person pushing changes direction and begins to pull, a posture alignment takes place and the hips are moved from a rear thrust to a pelvic thrust with the shoulders drawing back. See, as the spine changes position, the imaginary third leg of the triangle shifts through the body from the rear to the front. Knees bent, shoulder rearing back, the spine will now extend forward as if it extended to the floor.

"Okay these are basics of balance and people learn to do this when they are about nine months old. Not a great accomplishment in the whole scheme of things, but pretty impressive when you consider a pro running back slamming through the Denver Broncos' line and scrambling for a touchdown."

Terry "So we keep the nexus in our center and keep the nexus in the opponent's center? And then control where he can go with our movement?"

Linden "Close, but no cigar; actually, real close. You maintain the nexus in your center and take your opponent's balance by leading him to the missing third leg of that imaginary triangle. You move the nexus away from his center and then towards the forward or rear position created by his two feet and where the third leg of a milking stool should be. Look here, watch as the relationship becomes clear"

I took out a pen and sketched this diagram on a bar napkin.

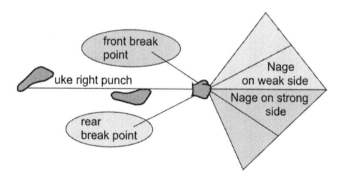

Linden "Now let me show you the relationship between this attack position and the triangulated stance of *nage*. I then drew this diagram on another bar napkin.

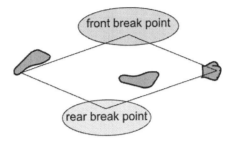

Linden "See, it makes sense if you look at the *uke* attacking with a punch and then look at the intersection of the fist and the forward defense posture of *nage* when they connect. Strong side to the left or weak side to the right, there is a direct relationship to the break point."

Ron "What if he moves his feet?"

Linden "Aye, there's the rub! Not if, actually, but when he moves his feet. You must be able to control the direction and time his steps and speed so that when you are ready and he has been manipulated to a place where he no longer has control of his center and direction, you can place him where you want. Either a throw or a pin would work then."

Ron "So the trick is to join the attack - and we call that junction the nexus. We have to be in our center, the nexus is in our direct middle, right in front of us. We lead the attacker's center to the point where he isn't centered. Right? Then throw him or pin him."

Linden "Almost. The attacker, or *uke*, attacks and will almost certainly be outside his center at the moment of joining. Think about the dynamic. If you strike with a *yokomen* or a right cross, at the moment of impact your hand is extended way away from you and you most likely would have one foot extended toward the person you are attacking. Take another look at the first diagram. In fact, at the moment of impact you are not lined up like a triangle with your feet and an imaginary third leg somewhere in front, but in a straight line. You are very easy to unbalance if your opponent understands the triangles and direction of travel.

"Think about a triangle. It is a very stable structure, right? Because of the way we evolved we learned to emulate the structure of a triangle to maintain balance. We do this by using our knees and shoulders to extend forward or back the balance that is needed to overcome momentum in any given direction. The best of us take it a step further and learn to mentally create a structure that uses both forward and rear balance, or break points, and they create a structure that emulates the base of a pyramid. The square. Most only use three points and that is why I refer to it as the milking stool. But the base of the pyramid is the most unmovable structure there is. That is Osawa Sensei. He utilizes both the forward and rear balance points and his two feet, combined with the nexus in his center. Moving him would be like trying to push one of the Great Pyramids.

"With your right hand extended forward and your right foot extended forward and your left foot in the rear – which direction does a *nage* need to push to make an attacker lose his balance? Toward either the front break point, that imaginary third leg of the stool, or toward the rear break point. Also, the imaginary third leg of the stool. What are the other two legs? The feet he is standing on…and what does he rely upon as the 'perceived' third leg…?"

Terry "The point of impact!"

Linden "Yes. *Uke* has to... he is in motion, by definition. That is the point we have described as the nexus, the point where *uke* and *nage* join. Whatever and wherever that is, that is the nexus and it is the most important point to remember if we are going to understand the implications of my little *satori*.

"We are now at this point where we have an *uke* attacking us. He is extended out with a strike coming at our head. We move, it doesn't matter where, and intercept the strike. That interception is the nexus. Done correctly it is directly in our center and it is in the process of being moved to *uke's* break point. We don't want *uke* ever to regain his strong position. Which direction do we move in order to get to *uke's* break point? To the imaginary third leg of the triangle either forward or in the rear.

"Now, truthfully, I have been aware of this for years. Nothing new here. What happened to me in D.C. at Cherry Blossom was the realization that while *uke* has to rely on the third point for his center and balance, especially during attack, *nage* was equally reliant on that point. For some reason, I had never seen the connection between *uke* and *nage* as being equal.

"While *uke* is being led to his break point by *nage*, it is imperative that *nage* maintain not just the nexus in his center, but that he maintain the nexus in, and as, his third leg of the triangle. He must never move to a place that he is vulnerable to the flows of power available to uke during the process of his break down. That was the realization I had.

"For years I had been watching my different teacher's feet – that's where the magic really lies. I had been focused on how they were always in *uke's* center and always moving *uke* to that imaginary third leg of the stool. I had just never realized that while they were doing it they were keeping the nexus as the third leg of the stool. The point of contact, the nexus, is *nage's* point of triangulation and as such, is his strength.

"Philosophically it goes deep into O'Sensei's spiritualism because it lights up the connection between us all. It illuminates the connection that we all have with each other whether in combat, in friendship, or whatever. For some reason, over all these years I trained to find the center of the attacker and move it with technique. Then I learned that the technique was not the important thing, being able to take *uke* to his break point was the most important thing. Now I see that the connection between *uke* and *nage* is the important thing and that while the break point is important, it does not need to be met to have success in self-defense. You don't need to damage the *uke* in order to succeed in going on with your life unharmed. The way we succeed in that is by keeping *uke* on the path to the break point and the nexus in our, or rather as, our center. Eventually the conflict will resolve."

Our dinner arrived and we started eating. The fish was excellent, lightly blackened and the salad a blast of memory, just like my grandma would have made. Spinach, with a sweet vinegar dressing filled with bacon and chopped egg as tangy and satisfying as a country farm breakfast. We ate in silence and watched televisions playing sports events: basketball, hockey, and baseball. I grew up eating in front of a television and somehow it still seems comforting to have all the flickering images to glance at while I eat. That is just the way it was back in the fifties, growing up with a new medium. My parents banned it after a few years, but by then the mold was cast. Of course the converse is also true. I sit down to watch television and I get immediately hungry. The waiter took the dishes and we resumed our conversation.

Terry "Okay, how do all our Aikido techniques fit into this picture?"

Linden "Technique is how we learn to control the motion of the *uke* as he attacks us. It is a set of basic motions that gives us a way to practice leading *uke* to the break point. Sometimes it is very direct, as with a *kokyunage*. We come directly over *uke's* punch and *atemi* directly into his energy. That is very effective and it is very deadly. Not the kind of thing that would be construed as kindness or loving harmony, whatever, but those words only have meaning in the correct context. That entry – true *irimi*, turns the center over. Just flips it up and over. We direct the *uke's* energy from forward to the third leg of the stool in back. Watch the dynamic sometime and you will actually see it.

"Technique is about break points in the human body and the way to get *uke* to those points. You can train in technique with no understanding of the connection that I refer to as the nexus. You can train in technique with no regard to triangulation in posture or movement. You can train in technique without understanding the idea of the break point or the idea of balance being triangular. People do it all the time.

"The fact is, we all do it in the beginning. All we do is train in technique. Once an individual starts to get beyond the basics, and for most that's somewhere between *nidan* and *sandan*, then we can start to focus his training on the principles behind why he does the techniques and he actually begins to learn what Aikido is about. Until then he is just practicing movements not unlike a karateka with his *kata*, or a dancer with his steps.

"I know that no one wants to hear that. It takes so long to get there. That is why we are having these conversations. I want you to become aware of the eight elements of mastering Aikido and to start employing them in your training."

Ron "Eight elements? Could you go over that, please?"

Linden "Okay, the first is to always keep the nexus in your center. The second is to always be aware of *uke's* feet, his triangulation. The third is to always be aware of your own. Basically, it is this: the nexus, break points, timing, technique, center, strategy, triangulation, and ki. There are lots of sub-routines I could introduce here. Things like never allowing the nexus to become important to your balance and well-being. Never allowing the nexus to become important in any way. Always being ready to break it off and find another point of connection – lots of different variables, but these eight will get you on your way to actually mastering this art. Oh, and one other thing that is very high up there on the list is to never allow *uke* to regain his center. Once we own it, we never give it back. If we do that it becomes wrestling, boxing, combat, or worse. The ninth element, humility, is so rare that we probably don't even need to mention it. It is not important in the martial sense, but in the spiritual sense."

Terry "How did the boxers utilize this knowledge? Or were they operating under a different set of rules?"

Linden "They were not at this level. They were extremely extended, utilizing enormous ki energy in their combat, but since their intent was to score points or to bludgeon their opponent half to death their only relative acknowledgement of this concept was the way they always kept their opponent in the center of their attack zone – their center, if you will. I don't think you can compare what they do to what an MAI does in his practice."

Ron "MAI?"

Linden "Master Aikido Instructor. My term. My wife, Laurie, used to be an MAI - Member of the Appraisal Institute. It is a fairly prestigious appellation and I used to joke with her that it meant Master Aikido Instructor. Just family silliness. But I got to like it since so many people don't understand the concept of Shihan, and that it really refers to your ability to teach and lead rather than your ability to perform Aikido. These clarifications are just some of the changes that I think are necessary to make Aikido more a part of the whole world. I think that is what O'Sensei wanted. From what I have read I get the feeling he wanted Aikido to spread out and be a means of world peace.

"Thankfully, the Ueshiba family has turned it into a world business. Please understand that I don't begrudge them this. They have held the art together and kept a level of competence that is recognized worldwide. They have sent fine instructors to all parts of the globe and we should be eternally grateful for their willingness to carry out the tasks necessary to keep this going. They have managed to unite disparate organizations and keep a semblance of unity amongst what could have become competitive organizations. Still, in order for it to become a worldwide art someday some changes are necessary and these few English clarifications that I use might become my part in helping the process happen."

Terry "Like using the terms nexus, break point and triangulation?"

Linden "Exactly."

Ron "What other sub-routines...hey, that's another one! Sub-routines. That's computer-speak. Did you just apply it to Aikido theory?"

Linden "Yes. I like it. I like the idea of installing programs, reformatting our hard drives, shifting our file systems from FAT16 to NTFS, reconfiguring operating systems...you name it. A lot of this can be applied to learning theory and it makes good sense. When you teach a technique, what are you doing but loading a new program? When a *nidan* starts to understand that the techniques he has been training are merely shadows of the reality that is Aikido, doesn't he begin to reconfigure his hard drive from one file system to another, or at least defrag the system in order to make it more efficient? Ron you are a systems engineer, both in hardware and software. Do you see what I am getting at? Terry, you are a systems engineer too, come to think of it."

Terry "Well, aside from the organic limitations and advantages of being human, I understand what you are saying very well. I don't think it really applies realistically."

Linden "No, of course not. But when you say that someone does something that is really 'cold', you don't mean that he went into a deep freeze to cheat his buddy or whatever it was that he did. Expressions are meant to help us get a hold on an idea or fact that might be otherwise slippery. That's all, and in that regard I like the idea of installing a few new programs in my student's Aikido operating system. By the way, I happened upon a theory from one of the medical school publications that espoused the idea that when children go through puberty they actually change the way that their brains file and process information."

Terry "Wow! That would explain a lot! One day they are cute nine-year-olds and the next they are crying and nobody understands them and they want to die right after they have killed everyone, if they can stay focused long enough."

Ron "Yeah, I asked my nephew one day if he was going to cut the grass and he looked at me and said 'I think it's four or five.' What? What the... But he really didn't connect the words I was speaking with what was coming out of his mouth. So there may be something to that. In fact it makes a whole lot of sense. If they start with a simple FAT16 file system and then try to reformat it into an NTFS system...only they have to do it while still using the same operating system...and while normal programs like eating, breathing, and going to school are still running...not to mention things like 'what to do with these sex drives' they never noticed before. I don't think we have ever invented a computer that could do that and still run."

Linden "It almost makes you feel sorry for them. All those teenage years, going from one half installed program to another, waiting for the whole thing to finish, to get caught up. It really does explain a lot. I'm glad you guys like the theory because I believe that something like this also happens when you get to where you are in Aikido. After a certain point, you have to rearrange all the information that you believed that you had understood. You have to relearn how to learn, what to look for, what to focus on, what to emphasize, what to strive for, and what your goals should be.

"Aikido builds like a mountain. You walk up the slope, it gets steeper and steeper, the way gets rocky and sometimes the ground slides around like a slope covered with loose mud. You begin to see daylight ahead, the path begins to lose its angle and suddenly you come around a corner and the path is level, maybe even slightly down hill. God, that feels so good after a long hard climb! But before you know it you are going downhill too fast and you find yourself scrambling for places to put your feet. You grab walking sticks and barely make it to level ground again only to find that the path begins up all over again. And this time the mountain is not some silly, third *kyu* foothill, but one of the big forteeners in the Rocky Mountain cordillera.

"Well, if you try real hard you can beat that puppy, too. And if you stay, well, one day you might even get a shot at one of the big boys, Ama Dablam, K-2, Cho Oyo, one of the world's real big mountains."

Terry "Did you summit any of the big ones when you trekked through the Himalayas?"

Linden "No, it isn't even something I'm interested in. But remember that we regularly climbed higher than the highest peak of the highest mountain in all of North America. My point is that all along you thought you were climbing mountains in order to get somewhere. Then one day someone like me comes along the path and you realize that I'm not wearing shoes. You stop and look and in a brief flash you see that I'm not carrying any climbing gear. A bit further on you notice that I have a pack of cigarettes in my pocket. And after a really ridiculous hard climb you come around a bend and find me eating noodles with some ancient Nepali porters in a little outside garden next to a three thousand year old chorten. Get it?"

Terry, Ron "No." "Uh, not really."

Linden "I am no longer following the rules of the climb, of the expedition. I'm barefoot. I'm drinking a cold beer. I'm relaxed. You have placed so many expectations on the climb, the way you do it, the mountaineering gear, the guides, the way the path climbs up and down, that you have lost sight of the true goal.

"The goal was never to get to the top of any damn mountain, it was to live your life while you were climbing. And to do it in the best way that you can. To meet all challenges in your center, to keep adversity at the nexus of your consciousness, with you, part of you, but away from your own center. To move through life with purpose, but lightly, leaving no mark on the mountain.

"A Sensei should be much more than an Aikido master. Once you get to the point when you begin to understand and master Aikido you are forced to realize that Sensei has been guiding you through your lives, not just on the mat. This is beside the point and not relevant to the focus of this discussion, but I think it is relevant that you don't even see this until you begin to change your file system and understand that training has really very little to do with technique. It has a great deal to do with understanding the principle we have been discussing. Which brings us back to the first question that you asked."

Terry "I don't even remember, Sensei. What was it? Something about ki, or the nexus?"

Linden "You asked about the center and why we keep the nexus there."

Terry "Yeah. That's right. I asked about keeping it in our center, just below the navel like we were always taught to be aware of our one point, there. Is that the same thing?"

Linden "No. But that is a very technical question and before I go into it I want to give one more short example of what we have been discussing. When I began playing guitar I learned many songs. I was not a very good guitarist yet, was just beginning. Over the years I learned more and more songs and played them better and better. It got so that I could just slip through the music and play what I wanted, easily, at will, however I felt it should be at the time. One day someone asked if I knew, oh, say... Blowin' in the Wind. That old Dylan tune. I did and played it...exactly like I did when I learned it thirty-five years ago. I had never re-learned it at the level of my current playing. By the third verse I was adjusting and adding, letting chords shift and change with the subtle nuances of the melody, but at first I was right back there again in 1965, doing my best to get my fingers to play the right positions.

"I know many Aikidoka who are like this. As their understanding grows their technique remains static and does not progress with their knowledge. I don't mean that they don't look good and have abundant new techniques, weird stuff with lots of *atemi-waza* and what not. They do. But the basic form of the fundamental techniques has not grown with their understanding. This is a problem, but only of laziness. They just need to work harder to raise their proficiency. It happens to many instructors, especially."

Terry "Are you trying to tell us something?"

Linden "No. Let's look at this idea of keeping the nexus in our center for a few minutes. What do we mean by 'our center'?"

Terry "I always thought that referred to the spot about two inches directly below the navel. That's what we learned back in the eighties when I trained at a Federation *dojo*."

Linden "Okay, that refers to something different. What I mean when I say 'center' is the space that is directly in front of you about four to eight inches out. This space differs in everyone but generally it is anywhere from three to six inches wide and can range from the knees to the head in height. Looking from the head down it is right here."

I grabbed a napkin and drew this.

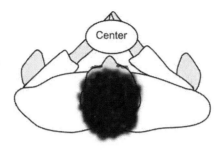

Linden "See if you let your arms hang by your side and then raise them up and bring them together you will be right there. But, come on, you guys know where this is. It's the place where techniques work. It's the place where, even if you have every other thing perfect – if you aren't there, nothing works. Why? I believe that it has to do with counterbalancing our butts, if you want the truth."

Everyone Laughing.

Ron "Okay, you have to explain that."

Terry "No, wait. I get it. Sensei's right!"

Linden "I believe that point of contact with *uke*, the nexus, is the front point of our triangle of balance. Because we are controlling the attack and leading *uke* about we can maintain our balance in motion. We do this by virtue of maintaining the nexus in direct relation to where our posterior is not. Exactly opposite, in fact. As we extend out – as we lean or turn away from our center, our butt goes out the same ratio in the opposite direction. Pay attention to your body shape as you move through techniques. If you keep the nexus in your center you are extremely powerful. The further you get from the center the weaker you are, because the nexus is further from the balanced mass created by your butt. Gee, I hate to be so analytical. I know you would rather be told stories about *samurai* and *katana* battles and the legends of old *bushido*, but the truth is far less glamorous. It is about human physiology and balance, speed and technique."

Ron "None of this has anything to do with being a warrior anyway, does it? I mean, a person's heart is the important thing. You can be a moral person without going to church and be a warrior without studying a martial art. What you are describing is how to master Aikido, and that doesn't have anything to do with culture or traditions. Right?"

Linden "Right. We are talking about mastering Aikido. And that means understanding how the body works when in motion. It is about how, and where, an *uke* attacks and how his center is compromised in the process. How we can assume control of his center and how and where we lead him so we can break his balance.

"The nexus is what we must maintain in our centers. The nexus is that connection that shifts and changes as *uke* moves through his attack. He might begin with that big punch with the right hand. Say we move to his right and bring up our own right hand and we deflect the punch at his wrist. As we do this we shift our hips to the left and rotate our body so the nexus – the junction of wrists – is directly in our center. We then begin the dance. The back and forth dance that we do when we capture *uke's* balance and lead him to the break point. Do we continue our spin and try for *kotegaeshi*? Do we continue the motion of our wrist and move him to his front break point and *ikkyo*? It doesn't matter, really. What matters is that we keep the nexus – the contact point – in our center and keep him off balance until he breaks off or down. If we do this we succeed.

"Now what about a second punch? What if he throws a quick jab and then follows with a right? The nexus changes, but the principle doesn't. As he shifts and continues, we move and continue keeping him in our center and looking for the break point in his balance. Sometimes we enter – *irimi* – just as he attacks and the collision is directed to one of his break points. This is *atemi waza*. We don't just strike. We strike to a direction. Here look." I drew this on another napkin.

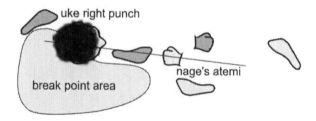

"You see, if you use *atemi*, the strike has to be in the angle or direction of *uke's* break point. Look at the diagram and you can see that *nage* has slipped inside the fist and entered into *uke's* space. He continues to enter with a somewhat triangulated stance and drive toward *uke's* head."

Terry "So the nexus is where?"

Linden "The nexus is the point of contact. The *atemi*."

Ron "But it isn't in *nage's* center."

Linden "Yes it is. Look."

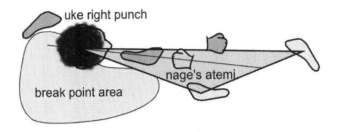

I shaded in the area representing *nage's* triangulated stance. "You know it isn't always perfect. We're talking human beings here and the resolution of the attack took about one third of a second. The nexus is the point where uke and *nage* meet. You know, sometimes it doesn't even manifest itself physically. Sometimes it is a look or an intimation of a touch. Sometimes it is a near miss. But it is always in *nage's* center and it is very real."

Terry "Well, once we have the center concept mastered so that we do all our technique in this center and we keep the contact – the nexus – always in the center, is that all?"

Linden "No. But it is a hell of a good start. Just understanding and realizing that in all your training, technique and daily life will take you up to about *yondan*. After that you need to begin really understanding triangulation. That will be another night. I'm going home. Goodnight.

Ron Sensei, one last question, please. Are there different kinds of energy or is it all about human force?"

Linden "Ron, the nexus in aikido is the point where two human energies meet, but it is not the only energy form present. This is probably the one glaring omission on the part of most teachers, so listen carefully. Aikido is, by definition, the act of nage extinguishing uke's attack energy. If nage adds energy to the mix, he is, by definition, attacking uke and then we violate the idea O'Sensei laid down. See, if nage really cranks up his energy level he is adding fuel to the fire. But aikido is the act of entropy. We disperse and extinguish attack energy. How? If we are to lead uke without increasing the energy output, we have to understand the laws of motion. An object in motion tends to stay in motion unless acted upon by an outside force.

"So if the laws of motion are correct, and as nage we cannot increase the energy level, what is the energy force that acts upon uke diminishing his attack energy?

Terry "Gravity."

Linden "Exactly. Gravity acts as an engine that constantly grinds us down and we spend all this energy constantly fighting it. Nage leads Uke to the point where he can no longer fight gravity. Gravity does it for us. We have the choice to lead uke there gently... as in ikkyo, or we can let gravity flush the energy with something like irimi-nage, just a huge energy dump. However we do it, we need to understand that the nexus leads, then gravity takes over. Only the very arrogant believe they are the power behind the fall. Understanding this is the beginning of humility.

"I have never liked seeing a sensei throw an uke in a high fall where uke has to slap the mat and then go through all the histrionics of amazement and faux wonder. Aikido done properly is very uninteresting. It is boring. It is just one attacker constantly grinding down to a point of no motion. Done well, nage is pretty boring. Most aikido instructors are desperate for recognition of their prowess and throw their partners all over the place and thereby demonstrate they haven't got a clue what aikido is all about. But they need the praise and the admiration and the stroke of their ego. As long as you understand these things, you can enjoy the show, it can be entertaining, but don't get caught up in the idea that they know what they are doing. They don't. Only study of the dynamics of the universe can teach you the true mysteries. Gravity, electricity, fusion and fission, and chemical reaction are the only kinds of energy there are. Don't get confused by nonsense.

"Good night."

Mitsugi Saotome, Sensei, presented this certificate to Daniel Linden on December 15, 1981. It recognizes the direct succession of Aikido instruction from O'Sensei to Saotome Sensei to Daniel Linden and grants him license to be a Professor of Shobu Aikido.

Mr. Linden received promotion to Rokudan, 6th degree black belt, from Hombu Dojo in 2005.

The Dialogs

Chapter 3

The Center

We met at the airport in Frankfurt in May of 2002, and drove through the quiet German countryside at 160kph. We had a chance to talk.

Arne is a friend who has built a fine *dojo* in Germany. I have one of his original pencil sketches on the wall of my dining room at home and often wonder how much care and concentration went into the many long hours needed for its creation. His life is a lot like that picture. He finds a way to balance his life with a serious career in engineering for an international corporation, a lovely wife (also an Aikidoka), and their precocious, stunning daughter, as well as run a *dojo*. He does it all with meticulous attention to detail and a soft, but firm, hand.

Arne "Sensei, I am so happy to see you here in Germany. Everyone is anxious to meet you and train with you."

Linden "Arne, I can't tell you how proud I am. You have accomplished so much in such a short period of time. Laurie sends her regards to you, and of course to your family."

Arne "Oh, well, yes. Thank you."

Linden "It really is a tribute to your perseverance and dedication that you have built this school so quickly and with so little help. To start a school is a massive undertaking and requires a powerful center. You must be like a rock."

Arne (embarrassed) "I don't know. I just see what needs to be done and try to do it as best I can."

Linden "Well, you've done a great job."

Arne "Maybe you should wait to see the dojo, first?"

Linden "I'm sure it is wonderful. Have you thought about what you would like to see for this seminar? Anything particular?"

Arne "Oh, well I would hope you would do what you feel is the right thing for us. You know European Aikido is not like what you do in America. Here, we do technique and technique and technique and sometimes a little more technique. Once in a while there will be ki training."

Linden "I thought I would spend the seminar teaching to recognize and use the center."

Arne "That would be wonderful."

Linden "There is a certain misunderstanding about the idea of the center that I would like to clear up so that we can begin building a bridge between the different pillars of what I call wisdom, or mastership. Most people think of the center as a place inside themselves or two inches under the navel or some novel idea like that."

Arne "It is what so many are taught."

Linden "True, but it is not accurate. To really understand the idea of the center we must first look at the way that human beings move. We stand upright.

We walk on two feet and unlike every other animal on the planet we have a pronounced rear end. It sticks out. You have heard me lecture at length on this subject in the past so you know to what I am referring.

"We are the only creatures on the planet with a butt. A posterior. We have this big mass of muscle and fat that acts as a keel like that on a sailboat. All other primates walk on four points and don't have butts. We developed them after we came out of the prehistoric forest and took to the savannahs. As the primeval forests shrank and the land gave way to vast savannas of grass the tree dwellers had to accommodate for their shrinking forage areas. They had to travel between the forests across huge expanses of grass.

"Anthropologists think that the more able a primitive human was to stand upright – and see over a savannah of grass - the more able he was to survive. He could see the lions, hyenas, wild dogs, saber toothed cats, whatever, and avoid them better. And therefore, breed. As the more successful primates began to stand upright the ones with the largest posterior were the ones most able to survive – and to use their hands for something besides walking. This allowed them to hunt. The theory is that the ability to use hands and to hunt increased the amount of meat protein in the diet and thus allowed the brain to increase in size. And here we are. We have big butts. There is an old joke that applies here. A man is walking through a jungle and encounters another man watching a lion. The lion sees them and starts towards them. The first man reaches down and tightens the laces on his shoes and says, 'I've got to be able to run fast.' The second man says, 'You can out-run a lion?' The first man says 'No, I only have to out-run you.' I think that is the way evolution works."

Arne "But how does that relate to the center?"

Linden "Here we are with these rather large posteriors. They act as counter balance weights to keep us upright and forward. And they work really well. What we describe as the center is the point opposite the posterior where we join with *uke* or a bit of work or whatever we are doing that needs us to perform at the highest standard possible. It is the place, to use internal combustion engine terms, where we develop maximum horsepower - where we are the strongest we can be."

Arne "How do we get there? Is there some special way to bring this about as we move? So often we must defend against a punch or some other strike that is not in our center, like to the side of the head, maybe? Or perhaps someone attacks in *ushiro-waza*, from behind? How do we find our center then, please?"

Linden "You need to understand that the center is flexible and it expands and contracts with circumstance. When we do that wonderful 'good morning' technique our center is the size of a hula hoop. The center is very large and it expands even more because we open our arms wide to expand it."

Arne "But from the rear, how do we, or can we bring this nexus to the center in front of us?"

Linden "Okay, let's take this one step at a time. The center is normally in front of us; about six to eight inches out and about even with the navel. It is maybe a foot tall, but can easily be expanded and it floats between the knees so if you are standing straight up with your feet together, it is very narrow. As your stance elongates the center gets wider as long as you keep it inside the triangle created by the sacrum in back and the kneecaps. It is very flexible, but once you try and move the action out of that triangle you are moving out of your center and the amount of power you have at your disposal begins to decline at an alarming rate. If someone attacks from the rear we almost always spread the floor, so to speak. We move into a larger space and often we extend our rear ends back into the attacker. This gives us more room to expand our center and it takes away the attacker's center by forcing him to lean forward over his knees and thus move out of his center."

Arne "I see. But sometimes, still, if someone is very strong and has taken you, how do you get it back? In *katatedori ryotemochi* for example, there are some who are so strong, you cannot move. There are some very large people who train here."

Linden "In the U.S. as well. But if you learn to move your center rather than the other way around, no one is too strong. Do you understand? You must move your center instead of moving your arms? This is one of the things that comes very hard for people who are young and strong and athletic. You can do so much just by moving your arms and shoulders. You are so strong that almost anything that we do can be accomplished by the feat of muscle strength alone. But if you are a small person, or weak, or old, or infirm, or sick, or injured...You know, even a strong man might get hurt in the first instant of a fight and then would benefit greatly to be able to be Aiki strong. Anyway, to be reliant on the muscle strength alone is a formula for disaster.

"Arne, there will always be someone stronger than you, someone bigger or meaner or more powerfully muscled. As big as you are and as strong as you are, once you find this place and master it, you will be amazing. You must turn your center to the nexus. Not the other way around. And then turn your center, with the nexus inside, to the attacker's break point. That is the source of my power and the place where I make magic."

Arne "It sounds so simple and I understand you perfectly as you say this. I understand and even teach this to my students. So why do you make this idea so special?"

Linden "You know Arne, I'm suddenly reminded of the parents who anguish for months over sitting with their adolescent child and telling him about sex, and when the conversation is over the child shrugs and says, 'Oh, I know all that!'."

Arne "Oh Sensei, please, I don't mean to make light of this, it is something I work on all the time."

Linden "I am sure that you do. You are a *sandan* and it is what you should be working on. You are my student and therefore it is something that has been taught to you for a long time. And also you are a teacher now and it is something that you should be aware of and teaching. All that being said, it is not something you have mastered. But it is one of the seven things that I believe one must work on consciously every day in order to achieve mastership. That is what I hope for you. To see you become a master of this art."

We pulled into a neighborhood in a lovely, small village that is surrounded by fields and stands of woods. The streets are wide and there is available parking on both sides, but the stores are only two stories high and seem to be quite old to me. As an American I am not used to buildings older than perhaps a hundred years. Here in Germany there are buildings that were built in the previous millennium. I look forward to meeting the students at the Aikido Dojo, Frankfurt.

Linden "Arne, the center is about more than the physical act of bringing the nexus to our power zone. It…"

Arne "Power zone?"

Linden "Yes, another term for the center. The place where we generate maximum power or strength."

Arne "I see."

Linden "The center also refers, at least metaphorically, to the sense of courage that we bring with us to life. I can't stress enough how our ability to face adversity calmly and with dignity, no matter the outcome, is a part of the warrior code. Think of the British sense of utter calm in moments of disaster. 'Uh, I say sir, you are on fire.' 'Damned uncomfortable, what?' It speaks well for a thousand years of knighthood and the code of arms. Or think of President George Bush when he came on television to speak of the September eleventh bombing of the World Trade Center."

Arne "I have seen his speech, not in full, but parts were in the news."

Linden "I don't believe I saw him blink once. His face was solid steel, no emotion, no openings. He was like Osawa Sensei when you are trying to attack him, simply an impenetrable wall. I was so proud. He demonstrated the strength and resolve of the American people more certainly than any amount of hyperbole ever could. You knew, just had to know, that he was dying to scream out his rage at the people who had done this thing. You knew that he wanted to break down in tears over the loss of our nation's people and way of life. But he never blinked. If a man ever attacked me with that kind of resolve I would make my stand, you know, *marubashi,* but I would be resolved to die.

"This is the kind of warrior spirit, calm and dignified in leadership, firm and resolved in war, compassionate and deeply committed to his religion and family, that exemplifies the greatest attributes of the American people. We suffered through almost a decade when the world saw us as insufferable, low class, parasites grubbing after McDonalds, Hollywood stars, and pubescent interns. But then, in our moment of greatest need, a man, a leader, rose up and showed the world that we are still a great people and that we still remember the warrior's code of conduct. This is now our nation's center. There are those who would destroy it, yes. But as long as there are some with the resolve to do what is necessary, we will persevere."

Arne "When I think of all that the German people have been through, the terrible things that were done, yet, the nation still moves forward. We grow stronger and more dedicated to a firm democracy and a just people."

Linden "Your center is still strong. That warrior code that has been around for a millennium is as strong today as it ever has been. You see movies like **Top Gun** and think of those young men flying at the speed of sound, defending entire armadas of ships and men and aircraft, battling one on one with other pilots armed with the power to destroy thousands. Think of the courage, the iron will, the utter and complete resolve to reach for victory or die in the effort. Think of the center those men must have."

Arne "When we saw the Americans destroying Soviet tanks during the Gulf War, how they could spot them miles away and destroy them before the Soviet-made tanks could even find where they were, I was amazed that back in the Cold War times, the East German tank crews were able to even think about going into battle with America. We discussed this quietly. No one wanted to admit that your tanks could be better than ours. We were told that we had the finest tanks in the world, but now we could watch CNN and see for ourselves."

Linden "That's right, I forgot that you were once the enemy."

Arne "Oh, you know, we believe what we are told and then things change. I don't think anyone ever thought of America as the enemy, only as the other side. It was very complicated. We were East German, yes, Soviet bloc, yes, but we were German first. And we could look through the gates and see the West. We knew that things were different. They told us about Western decadence, but when you are young? Decadence is not looking so bad..."

Linden "What you are saying is that through it all you kept your center as a people. It took a long time to put the country back together, but you did and now you can move forward as one united people."

Arne "Yes, we maintained our national center. Individual Germans never lost theirs. We suffered through many decades of despair before World War One and after. After the second disaster we were hungry and poor. There was no money and the eyes of the world were turned away from us, but the individuals who were determined to stay alive and go on, they held on to their hope and will. Each person contributes his own center to that of a nation."

Linden "You know the two bravest men I've ever known were my father and my stepfather. That's pretty strange when you think of it, but maybe my mother was attracted to the same things, deep down. I once watched my father – he was an off-duty police officer – walk into a bar after the owner had summoned him. The owner stepped out of the door and waved and my dad sighed and got out of our car. He'd been hired to wait outside and if there was any trouble he would be right there. Apparently there had never been any trouble or I'm sure he wouldn't have brought me along. He walked over to the bar door and marched on through. Arne, I don't think that that swinging door was even closed when he came flying back out through the air. He stood up and went back in and then other bodies started flying out."

Arne "Why were you there?"

Linden "My mom was having one of those parties women have where they buy make-up and then sit around and talk. It was no place for a ten year old boy to be, so my dad had brought me to this bar to sit outside in the car and keep him company."

Arne "So he won this fight?"

Linden "What happened was that the fight somehow got dragged outside. There were about six drunks all taking turns beating on my dad and my dad just kept hammering right back at them. One would go down and then another would take his place. I was stunned. I just couldn't believe that my father was taking such a beating and yet still fighting back, never wavering, never stopping, just punching and grabbing people and throwing them over the railing. Arne, it was a hell of a fight."

Arne "So he did win?"

Linden "You know, I never thought of it in those terms, winning or losing. It was more about survival or dying. Even at ten, I could recognize that. What happened was this; he got cracked over the head by one of those big, sixteen-ounce, glass coke bottles. He went down on his knees and then one of the drunks kicked him in the back and he flew face first down the steps. He hit the bottom and rolled and then got up on one knee. You could see that he was completely over this fighting nonsense and that he had given the drunks all the slack they were going to get."

Arne "He was angry?"

Linden "I expect that he probably was. When he came up off the steps he had that big K-frame Colt revolver in his hands and he was bringing it up to shoot somebody. And man, did they scatter, like a flock of birds. These guys disappeared like buckshot in a bale of hay. After a bit the on-duty cops arrived and they stitched him up right there. It was pretty weird sitting alone in the car the whole time. No one knew I was there. I had watched the whole thing from start to finish and when it was over Dad came back to the car and got in and we drove home like it had all been in a day's work. The only thing he asked me to do when we got home was get my mom to open the basement door, because he didn't want to walk through the women's party all covered in blood."

Arne "He was all right, then?"

Linden "My Dad was so tough, well, he was so tough. He has paid the price of being beaten, stabbed, shot at, and crushed in a deadly automobile pursuit. He aged hard, and though he is still alive, I think he would have been much more comfortable in his old age if he'd had an easier life. * My stepfather is aging hard as well, but he too, is still alive, although his people are not as long-lived as my father's. On the Linden side we live well up into our eighties."

Arne "Your stepfather, he was blind? Is blind?"

Linden "Yes. Watching him move around as a child taught me a great deal about center and ki. He could walk down the street and tell whether we were passing a house, a tree, a car, or an open field. I never figured out how he did it. He did have remarkable hearing, but he also had an intuitive sense of where things were that was beyond anything that hearing could possibly have given him. Blind people usually have their eyes open whenever sighted people do, and almost always move from their centers. It is really important to them that they never lose their balance.

* Author's note to the 2nd Edition. - Mr. Linden's father passed away after a long bout with cancer shortly after the First Edition came to press.

"You know, when a policeman wants to see how drunk you are or how much your balance is affected he asks you to perform something with your eyes closed. It isn't easy to keep balanced with eyes closed. So blind people learn to move from their center. My stepfather has arthritis now and it pains me to see how his sense of balance and touch are beginning to suffer.

"There was an interesting thing that happened to him many years ago. We speak of courage. We speak of center. I can't even begin to understand the amount of courage it took for him to do what he did. Every time I try to conjure up the idea of bravery I think of this.

"He was retired and staying at home a great deal. My mom is also blind, but has always been active and has taken advantage of many opportunities for group activities within her circle of friends and different associations. So she left him home alone occasionally and he would listen to talking books or the radio. He began to notice that things were missing. Little things. He found a pocketful of change gone from the top of his dresser. Then folding money. Then items began to turn up missing. When he asked my mom about these things she would not have a clue about them. Blind people are very careful about where they leave things. My mom has her place for her things. Dad has his place. And things were being moved or outright stolen.

"One day he felt the presence of someone in the house. You know the feeling, that you are not alone. He got up and turned the radio off and moved about the house, but could not find anything amiss or detect anyone. So he made a plan. The next time mom was going out he put some folding money on the table next to the bed, on the far side. Where someone would have to go around the bed to get it. He waited. Eventually he felt someone in the house.

"He detected a presence and did what he had done before. He got up and moved around and then made a show of stretching and sighing, and went into the bedroom where he lay down on the bed. Moments went by. Then he heard the dimes fall to the floor that he had folded into the bills and he lunged across the bed and threw himself into the thief. He wrestled him into submission and then called for help. It was one of the young people from the neighborhood. He would watch the house for my mom to leave and then he would rob it."

Arne "Unbelievable!"

Linden "Yes. You know Dad was a wrestler when he went to high school and I'll bet that he was pretty good. He was very strong and wiry and of course, had a terrific center. To this day I can't believe how much courage that took. I couldn't have done it. I know that. He didn't know that there weren't two or three. He didn't know if the thief was armed. He didn't know anything other than he was not a victim, and by god, was not about to become one. He took his life and destiny into his own hands and survived to become my hero. I've never forgotten what it means to be brave, nor where I learned it. And that is what I think of each time I think about being centered. My two dads. One a big brawling bear of a man and one quiet, reserved, and deadly certain. I am very lucky for both of them. They are the type of people who keep America centered."

We walk into the new dojo. It is just beautiful. There are flowers, carvings and pictures on the walls. It is austere, as it should be, yet warm and welcoming. Arne has done a fine job.

Arne "I have seen you move an *uke* away from you while he was stretched out all in a line and *uke* was right in front, standing strong. How is this to fit in your definition of centering?"

Linden "This goes directly back to the little *satori* I experienced back at Cherry Blossom in D.C. I am able to use the nexus as a point in my pyramid. I might stretch out and line everything up as you say, but in the instant that I make contact with *uke*, every one of *uke's* balance points becomes mine. It is quite remarkable. I was in Sensei's kitchen a few weeks ago and was explaining my English terms to him. He stood up and had me put my hand on his shoulder and push hard. He lifted me away effortlessly by moving through my center and directing the nexus to a break point. He did this while standing on one foot and leaning into me, and laughing. I was then able to re-direct him by adjusting my hip and bringing the nexus into my center. He was not amused and I really don't understand… I thought his whole idea was that his students achieve this understanding, but who knows? Anyway, by then we were just playing. He has total understanding of every nuance of balance, both *uke's* balance and his own."

Arne "So with Sensei, it does not count? Is he exempt from all rules?"

Linden "No, of course not. I said that I was able to re-direct, or rather, move him after he moved me. I think that was a great accomplishment. My observations of the principles even apply to him. He has the ability to practice these principles at the most extreme level, however. You understand that mastership has levels, too. If we say that O'Sensei was a master, what does that make Osawa Sensei? A master, too, that's what. If we say that Tohei Sensei is a master, then what does that make, say, Bill Sensei? Or Kevin? Again, still a master. Now, after that? Well then, we have lesser degrees of teachers, but there are people who are complete masters who are only *shodans*. I knew a man who had trained for thirty-five years, but completely disdained rank. I knew another who had received his *nidan* from O'Sensei, and chose to never be promoted again. They decided that teaching and being recognized as *shihans* was not important. But were they masters? Did they completely understand centering, triangulation, and break points. Did they embody the principles? Yeah, they did."

Arne "Can you give me an example of using centering outside the dojo?"

Linden "As you know I am a potter. When I wish to make something very large, anything over 12 inches high, for example, I need to use my full power to center the clay on the wheel. A piece that large might require fifteen or twenty pounds of clay, even more. To center twenty-five pounds of clay on a turning wheel requires strength, but also technique. You need to be able to put pressure on the clay body so that it moves into the centrifugal middle center. It must be enough pressure to cause it to rise up through the middle. It must be even pressure so the clay does not move to one side or the other and become unbalanced. Then, once it is high enough you must bring it back down in opposite movements until it is in an even flat-topped cone. To do all this I am very conscious of all aspects of centering in Aikido. I push from my hips while simultaneously bowing over the clay body. I bring the cone directly into my center, my actual body center. This motion is identical to *kokyudosa*. Once the clay has opened, that is, once I begin separating the core and making defined walls, I might stand and shift my feet so that I am triangulated to the work. Then I put the clay body in my center by moving the nexus, or connection, to my exact middle. I will use my legs to lower and pull, keeping the point of contact with the clay almost immobile in my hands. These are all Aikido principles and relate to the world directly through the clay."

Arne "It does sound exactly like Aikido."

Linden "Pottery is very similar in many ways. It is a remarkable pastime and art. What other endeavor can you pursue that utilizes earth, water, air, fire, and spirit?"

Arne "Spirit?"

Linden "Sure, creative spirit. I impose my creative will and turn earth and water into form, then use air and fire to refine it into something that will last for ten thousand years."

Arne "I never stopped to think about it like that."

Linden "A master potter uses the very earth for his colors, his power source, his structure, his form and even his inspiration and spiritual focus. I will never be a master potter, I am too interested in the technical and

I gave my best thirty years to Aikido. I do not have enough time left to conquer the mysteries of ceramics. I enjoy it, but that is all. I am competent but no artist."

Arne "Sensei, I like your work."

Linden "Oh, for sure, so do I! But it is not masterwork. I am not fool enough to think that anything I do is art. Well, perhaps my mandolins can be considered as art."

Arne "Your mandolins and violins are magnificent! And I have seen the photographs of your guitar, the maple arched-top. It is beautiful and certainly worthy of the term art.

Linden "I have never wanted to be an artist, only an artisan. I only wish to make usable, functional pieces that people can place in their homes and use until they break. I don't wish to be a wall hanger, at all. My art is on the Aikido mat. That is where my efforts to be centered have been for most of my life. Aikido is the filet mignon. All of the rest of my life is the mashed potatoes and gravy, the fine Burgundy wine, the fresh green beans and homemade bread and the ice cream at the end."

Arne "But without the potatoes and ice cream and all the rest you really don't have a complete meal. Does the filet mignon make the meal or do the other things make the steak a meal?"

Linden "All of life is a banquet. You are the only one who can decide with what you will sustain yourself. Only you can decide."

The Dialogs

Chapter 4

Defining Aikido

When you name me, you negate me.
Nietzsche

Thirty years ago I thought I understood Aikido; what it meant to practice it, to do it. I was naïve and a bit pretentious in my self-acknowledgement. I thought I knew all the important things and only lacked the divine inspiration. I wanted a *satori* or in western terms, an epiphany, to take me over the edge in understanding. I trained for years for that moment.

Learning all the basic techniques made me formidable. Hard training made me strong. Study of Judo and Karate, American boxing and *Tai Chi* gave me an expanded vocabulary and greater overall understanding of martial arts in general. I learned.

Along the way I met a man named Akira Tohei who understood that I was waiting for enlightenment. One day he said to me, "Dan-san, everybody wants a big *satori*. Everyone wants to touch the tree and see the earth and God and understand everything. That isn't what happens."

I asked, "Why not? It happened to O'Sensei." I was actually serious, not understanding anything, at all.

Tohei Sensei (he had been my teacher then for a few years) looked at me gently – though he was not a kind man – and said, "Dan-san, there are many little *satoris*. They add up over the years. They are like coins in a bowl, they build and build and build and then one day you realize you have money. You suddenly realize you can buy a new car or house or whatever you want – all the possibilities are open to you. But you gain this understanding through hard work and saving and over much time. Big *satori* is like that. Many little *satoris* all stored up and then one day you see something and it is like a brick in a wall that finishes it. It is like a game of *go* – one stone and the circle is complete. Go train harder."

"Is that what happened to O'Sensei?" I was referring to the legend of the battle that preceded the moment of his enlightenment.

"Oh, *hai*, okay, Dan-san, don't worry. There won't be swords." He laughed. "O'Sensei wanted to talk to this old friend, and you know he was a warrior, a retired admiral in the Japanese Navy. When he came to see O'Sensei they argued and the Admiral then took a *katana*, a live blade, and attacked O'Sensei. O Sensei moved about and when the Admiral attacked, he knew where the Admiral was going and how quickly and with how much force. It was easy for O'Sensei to avoid the attack and when the Admiral was exhausted and left, O'Sensei leaned against a tree in his garden and thought about what had happened.

"It was like that brick in the wall. Suddenly he understood. They say 'Big Satori', but it was really about filling the blank that was left. He saw, and then understood and was able to see the big picture – it all became clear..."

I said that I understood. Tohei Sensei was a considerate man and let me go then. That was more than thirty years ago. There have been many times since that I've been stunned by an understanding or a moment of clarity. I remember seeing *kotegaeshi* as a wrist throw and a specific technique. Another Sensei cured me of that one night after class when he turned out the lights and asked me to attack him by the dim glow of the red EXIT lights.

I struck and lunged and flew at him over and over and every time he threw me with *kotegaeshi* but he never touched my wrist. Not one time. He never touched my hand. Not once. I couldn't believe it and it was only years later that I truly understood the gift he had given me. He was showing me that the principle of *kotegaeshi* transcended the physical specifics of the technique. He demonstrated over and over that *kotegaeshi* is an archetypal form, a universal idea that is transcendent over any specific wrist grab or throw.

I sat later, exhausted, and asked him "Is that the way that O'Sensei taught you?"

"O'Sensei was not so kind. He was not so generous." He responded. "We had to steal his technique, steal his training form. He showed us many techniques, but only to demonstrate principle. He would show six or seven different things and *deshis* would jump up and try to do them. The thing that he was doing, though, was showing a principle and few ever saw that. You had to learn the principle and then steal the technique because he didn't care whether you learned that or not. The technique was not important to him because he was so far beyond that concept. He thought only in principles, but so few could grasp the principles… He was a very hard man.

"So many of us tried to find his secret, what made him so strong. He was old, you know and like a tree." Sensei leaned back and laughed a bit, then patted my shoulder. He left and I tried to understand the lesson. It was ten more years before I really had an inkling that the lesson had been about something more than my notion of "principle".

The years have been kind and generous. It was during the April 2003 Cherry Blossom Seminar in Washington DC – my Sensei's celebration of fifty years in Aikido - that one of the final bricks slid home in the wall. That is what this book is about. The secrets that make up the finished picture of what it is that we do when we reach a level of mastership in Aikido.

We were having a few beers after class one night when one of the new *shodans* asked me how long it would take before I felt he would be really competent in Aikido.

Linden "I think that the answer to your question is s*andan*, and only you will be able to tell me how long it will take for you to reach that level. *Sandan* means that you know all the basic techniques and that you can move from one to the next, smoothly. It means that you can think or rather respond without thinking and that you can perform at a level where you are competent. *Sandan* is about where most people really stop progressing unless they start their own *dojos*.

"Starting a *dojo* from scratch is really hard. You must think about every little thing in order to explain it to your new students. So if you don't start a *dojo*, you just keep doing the same things. To get beyond *sandan* without teaching, a person must think about technique a great deal and spend an enormous amount of time trying to understand the principle of not just the technique, but the theory of why the movement begat the technique. Not to get too biblical on you."

Mike "Why the movement begat the technique?"

Linden "Sure. The technique doesn't just spring into being without relating to movement or the need to respond. Technique is the result of human physiology responding to an attack from a certain quarter or place, with a certain velocity, and a certain strength. That is plain. Why would anyone go about twisting any old wrist unless he had a need to do this? The need arises when someone threatens him with a knife and he responds to the threat. *Kotegaeshi* is a normal movement when attacked by a thrust – the attack triggers the response. You would have to work pretty hard to get a *kotegaeshi* if someone slashed at you quickly and then retreated. Unless your hands are faster than mine, of course. Slashing attacks would trigger a different set of possible physiological responses. The speed of the slash, the angle, the power behind the slash – all these things are taken into account when a competent *Aikidoka* is attacked and responds. He just doesn't think about it, that's all. Being competent means that you respond without having to think about it.

"Mike, if you were attacked by a quick, hard, thrust – and I mean straight up the middle – what would you do? Don't think, just visualize."
Mike   "I don't know, Sensei. I guess I would just *tenkan* and *kokyunage*. You know, just join and come back."
Linden   "And you would be right. You see, the attack begat the technique. Such a great word, begat, it is really too bad we don't use it anymore."

We laughed a bit and watched the evening deepen through the overhanging bamboo and ginger. Across the yard I heard my dogs come bounding toward us, two hundred pounds of fur, teeth, appetite, and pure love. Typical Labrador retrievers, they jumped into the middle of us and found someone to lean on and someone to bother for pets. They finally settled down to some serious scratching and rolling about on their backs.

Curtis   "Are you saying, then, that all the techniques we practice are the only techniques?"
Linden   "No Curtis. Ultimately I am saying that there is no such thing as technique at all. I, well, anyone who is looking at Aikido from a perspective of mastership sees that technique is merely a language that we all agree on in order to practice movement against different attacks. The movements incorporate the principles that O'Sensei brought to us and called Aikido, but they are not Aikido. Aikido is training in an art that teaches us to move from a centered place, find the attacker's center and then lead that person to a place of imbalance. It is really quite easy to explain,

but very difficult to understand. The Japanese language and the mysticism that surrounds Aikido are used to control the flow of information and maintain the foundation of the mystical. But there is nothing mystical about what we do and there is no mystery. It is very difficult, however.

"I remember seeing Michael Jordan running up the basketball court and Charles Barkley coming over to defend him. Jordan was very respectful of Barkley's ability to defend a dribbler and slasher. He hesitated and then glanced over Barkley's shoulder. At that very instant he moved to the right while actually crossing over and moving to his left. Barkley's balance left him. He stumbled, tried to correct and could only watch while Jordan slashed up the middle and dunked the ball into the hoop. As good as he was, Barkley could not control Jordan's center. Jordan not only had complete control of himself – the thing that made him such a genius - but he could control his defenders with a mere glance."

Terry "I've seen Sensei do that. Stop Dennis or Lauren with a single, searing look. Sensei allows you to think you can attack, but then just glances at you and you realize that what you thought was an opening was really just an illusion."

Linden "Just like Jordan led Barkley to think there was something going on behind him and in this instant of hesitation took him to the hole."

Luke "Is Aikido just mental then, really?"

Linden "No, but there is a great deal of observation, decision making, strategy, calculation, and just plain guesswork that goes into controlling an attacker. Aikido's ultimate goal is really what? It is, very simply put, controlling an attacker. We use certain methods of control that are definable by Japanese terms such as *kotegaeshi, iriminage, or ikkyo tenkan* or whatever, but these movements simply translate into wrist throw, entering throw and technique number one. The purpose of these techniques is to control an attacker's movement. That's it. There is nothing mystical about it. All Aikido is, by definition, and this is really open to interpretation depending on who you ask, is the way of spiritual harmony. What the method is, by definition, is controlling an attacker. Some senseis can do it by merely looking at a person. Osawa Sensei could do it with no hands touching. Most mere mortals need to study and learn and practice until they have the ability to keep their center in place while moving the attacker to his weakest position. Really, that is a pretty good definition of Aikido."

Derek, a very large Canadian man originally from the Caribbean Islands, and a very accomplished karateka, wanted to ask a question. I could see he was troubled by this definition.

Linden "C'mon Derek, what's on your mind?"
Derek "I understand Karate. It is pretty well defined as the art of attacking and defending with kicks and punches, it means kara, empty –te, hand. Fighting empty handed. But I know that there is a real complex philosophy behind the art. I think a lot of people are attracted to Aikido because they perceive it to be an art or philosophy based on non-violence. You just defined it as a practice of movements without regard to the

intent or reason behind the movement. Or am I missing something?"

Linden "I am simplifying it a bit, I'll admit, but the real essence of what we do is not dependant on any philosophy or dogma. We need to adhere to some pretty basic tenets regarding intent and responsibility, but we could change the name of the art, wear pyjamas to train in and sing camp fire songs after each class and it really wouldn't change a thing."

Luke "Except there would be a lot fewer of us here!"

Derek "Can you take the Shinto mysticism and the non-violent philosophy away and still retain the true intent of the art, the dream that O'Sensei had?"

Linden "Derek, why are you not still training in karate-do?"

Derek "It was too violent."

Linden "For you, or as a way to resolve conflict?"

Derek "Both, I think."

Linden "And you came here hoping to find?"

Derek "A way that would allow me to express the level of violence needed but not to exceed it. If my brother took a swing at me... well, just one good kick in the head could hurt him. I'd never want that. I thought that with Aikido I could learn to control him without hurting him."

Linden "I rest my case."

Derek "Huh? What did I say?"

Mike "You wanted to learn to control him. That's what you just said."

Derek "No, I mean that I wanted to not hurt him. I would not want to hurt him. I don't know about control. You know what I mean."

Linden "No, go on."

Derek "What I mean is that if he got drunk, or angry – if he did something that required me to defend myself – I would not want to hurt him, so I would prefer to use an Aikido technique rather than a karate kick."

Curtis "Aikido techniques can easily kill or maim someone. Are you aware of that? There are a lot of techniques that are designed, well, designed to kill. There are no options for this. We train for three or four years to understand the concept of *ukemi* and then, as I understand it, a few more years before we're really competent. Someone who is not trained like this would be killed by *irimi nage* or *juji nage*. You do understand that?"

Derek "Of course. But we learn that we have the option to exercise how strongly we can do these techniques."

Curtis "Don't you learn to exercise how strongly you throw the kick or punch in karate?"

Derek "Okay, I get your meaning..."

Linden "No, actually you don't. You are making the classic mistake of confusing Aikido with Aikido technique. I guess we need to define what the difference is so that we can all move forward together. When I defined Aikido as maintaining our center while finding and displacing the attacker's center, I implied a great deal. That you understand what center is; that you understand where and how it is found; that you can actually lead that person to a place of imbalance; that you understand what and where that place is. The point is that the simple definition is based on a great deal of knowledge and training. Coupled with the knowledge and training is the basic philosophical tenet that elevates Aikido from all other martial arts - that moral conscience is important.

"Now you men hear me talk about the ethics of Aikido fairly often, but I almost never discuss the Zen, Shinto, or mystical associations that so many people define as 'Spiritual'. That's because I don't believe Americans need it. It doesn't relate to us and is completely foreign to our culture. That so many people want to make a religion out of this martial art is really a shame. They have forgotten that we already have perfectly good religions here and in place. How many churches do you pass on this street alone, just to get here? The problem is that so many people feel alienated from the orthodox religions and want to find some Star Wars type of warrior/religion to make their lives feel fulfilled. It is really sad. Now Aikido attracts these people in droves.

"During the seventies it was kung fu. Everybody wanted to do the kung fu thing, but when they found out how hard it is to be a Shaolin monk they just opted for shopping mall karate stores instead. Shaolin priests started small temples here and there and had all kinds of students ready to spend their lives as monks until the first time they were awakened at four thirty in the morning to scrub the dojo floors by hand and then to practice a couple hours before breakfast. Look at the temple over on Goldenrod Road. One of the truly great kung fu masters in the world lives there, but he is reduced to teaching a few *tai chi* classes and wondering where all the really dedicated students went.

"Now the focus seems to be on Aikido. The spiritualists latch onto what they like about Zen,

Buddhism, Shintoism and the like and of course leave out the stuff that doesn't fit their fantasy. But Aikido does not require us to be Buddhists. It only requires us to act with a conscience. It requires us to act morally. It requires us to see the attacker as our brother and to be our brother's keeper. These things we can do without trying to be latter day *samurai*.

"I am descended from Vikings, Black Irish rebels, and Teutonic warriors. We embrace a long and glorious warrior tradition that is in no need of shoring up from the East. That is why you don't hear me talk about the samurai code, *bushido*. We already have a warrior code. We don't need anyone else's. We'll talk about this later on. Right now I want to emphasize that the definition of Aikido must have this moral caveat or it is only Aikido technique that we practice.

"Now, there is another step involved as well. True Aikido is not bound by technique at all. The only purpose to teaching the classical techniques is to give us a common language and format to begin our training. Ultimately you will forgo these techniques or at least realize that they are only a beginning to understanding basic physiology and human dynamics. Now somebody find me a beer. Please."

We drifted into conversations about other things as we left the steps of the dojo. We walked through the expanse of day lilies, ginger, bamboo, and orchids that make up the garden around the dojo and up onto the deck behind my home. Finally we settled into a comfortable group looking out across the grounds bathed by the setting sun. The air was cool and filled with the scent of orange blossoms. Our big, old

Labrador retrievers landed firmly at our feet and both sighed in unison.

Derek "Sensei, I don't see why a karate style kick, if thrown without a lethal intent, couldn't be construed as Aikido, too. I mean, couldn't we use a kick, in, or as, a technique?"

Linden "Yes, of course. And we do. That's right, you haven't been here that long. Sometimes students fit in so quickly you forget they haven't always been here. Sorry. Yes. We do. There are some teachers famous for their footwork. I've seen Steve attack a Sensei with a *yokomen* and watched him catch the strike with the inside of his foot and knock Steve snap, right over into a hard fall. It's very impressive. My legs are so short I can't really do this, but I will be glad to teach the technique and maybe a couple of you will find you have a facility for this kind of thing. I think I just blew by your question, though. Were you asking, is karate the same as Aikido?"

Derek "No, of course not. I can see the difference."

Linden "Because if you were thinking that, you were more right than you can imagine."

Derek "What? That's not what I...."

Linden "But there is more to it. In the end, all techniques are the same. When you reach mastership, technique is formless, no style, no method – just the manifestation of the individual's personality and background. And Derek, it doesn't really matter if you kick hard or not in regards to intent. Now if I turn to Mike, who has many years studying Aikido, and ask him if he sees that karate and Aikido are the same he might say that he sees this. Do you Ron?"

Mike "Well, no. My brother practices karate and my children do as well and I don't see it."

Linden "Well Derek, Mike has been here for almost ten years and he disagrees with you. Do you see that karate could be the same as Aikido?"

Derek "I don't want to disagree with Mike, Sensei, but doesn't it all have to do with intent?"

Linden "Guys, let's look at this from a different perspective. Would a karateka see what we do as karate? Would an American fist boxer see what we do as boxing? Would a judoka see what we do as judo?"

Chorus "No, I don't think so." "No." "Not a chance."

Linden "And yet, I see what they do as Aikido. The differences are very telling, yes, but the point can be reached when all the movements of all of the many physical arts blend into one smooth flow from the heart and it is Aikido. Look, if I use a technique to ward off an attacker, and use it with the intent to do harm, is it still Aikido or is it *aikijuitsu*? Derek thinks it has to do with intent. He is right. A hard kick is nothing more than *atemi* if it is done with loving kindness, right?"

Derek "Sensei, I have the feeling you are being facetious. That remark about 'loving kindness' is a red herring if I ever heard one."

Linden "Okay, we're hitting on a lot of subjects here really rapidly and if we are going to make sense out of this we need to focus a bit on specifics. First, I define Aikido as moving an attacker's center to a place of imbalance while maintaining my own center. The process with which I do this is what defines most people's notion of what Aikido is. We practice a number of basic forms to train ourselves in ways to lead the attacker to a place of imbalance. For most people, these forms are Aikido.

"Now, the truth is that we learn these forms in order to have a common vocabulary with which to discuss the actual training – which is the study of the principles of Aikido. How do we achieve and maintain the nexus, that point where all contact is focused and from where all movement is initiated? That is the true study of Aikido. All the rest is superfluous.

"By this definition, if you focus on what I just said, you could achieve mastership in Aikido by training in karate, boxing, judo, *aiki-juitsu, tai chi, kung fu,* ballroom dancing, basketball, or just about anything, assuming you had a master instructor to guide you. The trick would be getting everyone who trained with you to give up the goals of the endeavor and focus on the principles of Aikido or the principles of mastering movement in general. And what would be the point of that? In basketball the point is to win the game. In competitive ballroom dancing, well, I guess the point is still to win. All these endeavors have a different goal than Aikido, which is to achieve understanding and mastership of human movement in the realm of self-defense.

"I am discounting all the philosophy of the art because I want you to understand that mastership can be achieved with no reference to intent. However, I truly believe that if a person does not actually embody the heart of true Aikido intent, he would quit long before mastership merely because he would not need to achieve it for any other reason than his own ego or self-image. He would need to already be an ethical individual that embodies the mind of Aikido before he could reach mastership. It is just too difficult a path to pursue for any other reason."

Curtis "You're saying that an unethical person could not become an Aikido *shihan*?"

Linden "Clever, Curtis. No, becoming a shihan is often more about how well we perform politically in the organizations that oversee the business of Aikido. Please remember that the rank of shihan equates with the title of Professor. This is not the same thing as a working Ph.D. You hold a Ph.D. in electronics, but you are not a professor. Which is better? Does a professor know more about electronics than a man who spends his life designing guidance systems for the space shuttle? I don't know. So I've been talking about reaching mastership of Aikido. Not becoming a shihan. The two are often one and the same, but not always. My friend Dennis is a fine example of someone who is both shihan and who has reached mastership. There are others here in Florida.

"What I am specifically saying is that it requires an ethical individual, one who already lives by the Aikido rules of conduct, to have the courage, fortitude, wisdom and perseverance to stay the course throughout all the years of hardship and struggle to become a master of Aikido. In other words, we don't need no stinking batches."

Everybody laughed at my impersonation of the old movie character Pancho Villa except young Jeremy who typically said, "I don't get it."

Mike (With thick Mexican accent) "What Sensei means, is that you can study all the spiritualism, and Buddhism and Shintoism you want, but all you need is a fundamental core of morality and ethics to be what O'Sensei wanted us to be. You don't need no stinking spiritualism."

Jeremy "I don't get the accent!"

Mike "It's from the old westerns - from when the Mexican bandits would pretend to be Federales and then stop someone to rob them. The people would ask to see their badges and they would always say 'we don't need no stinkin' batches!' oh, never mind. "

Linden "All right, all right. Jeremy, I don't want to seem flippant, but it is really important that you don't take any of this too seriously. I am just trying for a laugh. We have a long road before us and sometimes it's important to remember that a laugh with people we care about is a lot more important than an idea someone had about something three hundred years ago. Especially an idea of spiritualism from a culture that no longer exists. Especially trying to assimilate that cultural understanding. So I made a joke. It is only important that you understand that O'Sensei charged all his students with making the world a better place. He told us to 'protect and defend all living things'. There is a tradition of that in Christianity, and Judaism. You are Jewish, right?"

Jeremy "Yes."

Linden "If you went to your Rabbi and asked him if you should be kind and treat all people as your own brothers, if you should defend life even when someone is attacking you. What would he say?"

Jeremy "He would say yes. We've even had this discussion."

Linden "Okay. You don't need no spiritualism."

I heard my wife clear her throat from behind me. Busted. She is always trying to tell me to be more dignified with the students – doesn't like my sense of capriciousness.

Lauren "Instead of quoting Pancho Villa, why don't you quote O'Sensei?"

Linden "Like what?" I asked.

Lauren "Well, for one, that quote about protecting and defending all life. What was the entire quote? It is one of the most profound things that you regularly use around here. Or did you forget it?"

Linden "Okay, you mean the quote titled *Take Musu Aiki*. Sure. Do you guys know it? Haven't I recited it a bunch of times?"

Lauren "Dan, I don't think I've heard you go through it since the last big *yudansha* test, when Terry and Nick went for *nidan* and Mike tested for *shodan*. That's been about four or five years ago."

Linden "You're right. Koichi Tohei Sensei spent a lot of time discussing this when he first came to the United States over twenty-five years ago. Here goes. O'Sensei said "You and I and everything in this universe exist as a part of the endless flow of God's love. Realizing this, we recognize that all creation is bound together by the same benevolence. To harmonize with life is to come into accord with that part of God, which flows through all things. To foster and protect all life is our mission and our prayer. We call our path *Take Musu Aiki*." Personally, I have always found it interesting that he decided to call it *Take Musu Aiki* and not Aikido. I'm not sure of the exact translation, but he differentiated between the spiritual path and the study of Aikido and I think that that is what is important."

Everyone sat quietly for a few minutes. There is a time when silence falls upon a group, and the collective consciousness becomes aware of itself for an instant. That group experiences unity. When I was in Viet Nam we would be out on the rivers or jungle and the Chief would stop us and we would all know, collectively, what we were about and where we were going. We would be aware of immediate danger and know what was necessary to protect us and to achieve our goals. Other times it was havoc, pandemonium, or just plain chaos, but I do remember several instances when that group mind expressed itself and those times stand out in my memory as the strongest recollections of the war. For an instant, I felt this again as we sat there in the growing dark, the sighing of the dogs welcome in the flickering light of the candles. Then someone popped the top on a beer and the moment slipped away.

Mike "Did you say, 'take a moose to Aikido?' What?"

Terry "Why do you think that your sensei quit going over that with his students?" He really doesn't spend too much time discussing any of the spiritual concepts anymore. Not like he used to, maybe ten years ago."

Linden "I think it's a combination of two things really. The first is that he expects us, his senior staff, to do this for him with our students. And second, he has come to understand that Americans are a spiritual people with a great warrior tradition of our own. Has anyone here ever taken an oath 'to protect and defend' something, 'so help you God'?"

Tim "Yeah, when I joined the U.S. Army."

Terry "Me, too."

Curtis and John "Yeah."

Linden "'To protect and defend the Constitution against all enemies both foreign and domestic', is what the oath says, if I'm not mistaken. The Constitution of the United States, being the greatest protector of human rights in the history of the human race, is a nice stand-in for O'Sensei's 'To protect and defend all life'. Do you get my drift? I think that Sensei has understood over time that Americans are generally a moral, ethical people and he just doesn't have to hammer the spiritual side of Aikido. We're already there or already getting there."

Curtis "Well then, does Aikido require a spiritual foundation in order to be Aikido as opposed to aiki-juitsu?"

Linden "I'll answer your question with a question. Can an atheist and an immoral, unethical individual practice Aikido?"

Silence lasted longer this time. I could tell the men were thinking about individuals that they had known over the years. Remembering stories of deeds done and things said. Wondering if these acts and words fell into the categories mentioned. I know how I felt and knew that I was treading water in the deep end of the pool. There is a fine line that one can draw that makes others step one way or the other, and you need to know where they will step before you draw it.

Linden "Of course they can. One of the core beliefs of all religions is the concept of rebirth. To be made whole, again. To be washed clean. That one may rise above all adversity and find peace and fulfillment in the philosophies that the religions embrace. We need to be careful not to cast the first stone when we might be deserving of an avalanche. It doesn't matter if a person is not deserving when he makes the first step into a place of higher thought, only that he strives to become worthy."

Derek "Sensei, it sounds like you are describing Aikido as a religion to me."

Linden "Well, damn, it does sort of, doesn't it? Trust me, it isn't. But it is certainly an endeavor, not unlike theosophy, which expects every participant to be an ethical and moral person. I believe that it is implied that a student of Aikido is a person on a path to better him or herself. It doesn't require that the discipline be Eastern.

"So often I find myself explaining these things, these fine lines, these definitions. The really important thing to always remember is that training contains the only truth. Only by sweating and rolling around and struggling to give up all that masculine muscle do we ever get to the magic and face it, the magic is what we really seek. I have had a lot of students over the years that finally told me, on quiet, tired and sometimes drunken nights that what they are really training for is to find and master *ki*. The only way is train, train, and then go train some more.

"And with that I will bid you all good night."

The Dialogs

Chapter 5

On Spirituality

Dennis Hooker sat playing an old Gibson 5 string banjo. He was playing in the style known as "claw hammer", an ancient form that came long before the current blue grass style. His timing is a bit skewed. His syncopation is not that of a young fire brand, but he has a simple magic that catches the eye of the crowd and makes the kid's faces light up like a roman candle. He is happy. Dennis has found the contentment that is shared by so many people who play instruments and make music, not for the big crowds and nightclub groupies, but for themselves. Like a kind of backwoods *kotodama* with the sounds echoing off the undersides of the leaves and the soft evening breeze... people join in. A guitar materializes, soon a mandolin, then a tambourine.

He sips a glass of wine. No more beer for this veteran of the bar wars. He is content to taste in the wine the subtle hint of eucalyptus and currants and ripe plums. Like everything in his life, his palate has matured. He rises more slowly, falls less often and has an easy grace that others admire, but rarely understand. He is a Shihan. He is also an Aikido Master. The two are not always synonymous, but in his case it is a fact.

He is my friend. He is someone I trust completely. What more can you say?

We were celebrating the tenth anniversary of Shoshin Aikido Dojo. A huge crowd came and moved around us as we sang songs and celebrated the day. Ten years. Think of it. Dennis had been there ten years before when the storm of the century had blown and broken trees and sent outbuildings crashing and bashing their way across the open ground. He had stopped over to see how I had made it through. I was standing in the crushed and shambled remains behind my home, staring at the devastation when he said, "If you build it, they will come."

I said, "That's a line from a movie."

Dennis said, "It doesn't make it untrue."

"I guess not."

"What do you need?"

"Some stakes, some string, a one hundred foot rule."

"Got 'em?"

"Yeah. I guess so."

"Go get 'em."

So I did.

He had known what I was thinking about as only a close friend could. We started out looking for the best lay without taking out any more trees. We were also concerned with the sight line of the house, but eventually settled on how we could put the *dojo* up without taking any more trees than necessary. I already knew that I would call it Shoshin Aikido Dojo. We drove stakes, set up batter boards and then drew string and started measuring. After a while I realized it was hopeless and decided to have someone come over who had actually built a building before. We did leave the stakes, batter boards and strings in place. When I finally built the dojo I ended up using three of the four spots that Dennis and I had surveyed for the corners. I had to move one for the sake of having a square building. I had never built a building before and it was a good thing no one came along and told me how hard it was going to be, because I probably would have quit right then.

Twenty years later we are still playing together, still doing Aikido together like old men, and occasionally fishing together. We wish we could fish more, but when you get old it seems harder and harder to get out. It's too cold, hot, rainy, dry, muggy, foggy, far, near, deep or shallow. Sort of like life.

Hooker "Linden, do you ever get to hunt quail anymore?"

Linden "No, I had all kinds of plans to buy and establish coveys all over these different hunt camps and maybe even in some public lands. I'd only tell the landowners and keep the locations of the coveys to myself, but they always disappeared. Up in Maine we hunt partridge, though, and there are enough so that you can really find them anywhere. The dogs don't quite get it though, and I'd like to find some to train them with. How are you supposed to have bird dogs without having birds?"

Hooker "I keep wondering that myself."

Linden "The truth is, I just don't have the time or energy to plant cover and go out and seed areas, then get someone to clear cut and burn and then do it all over again. Let alone actually buy birds and go out and establish coveys. Man, when you get done doing all that and then factor the price of a quail dinner… Well, I don't know."

Hooker "Makes a three dollar chicken taste awful good, don't it? The only reason I care any more is for Dooley. He's a born and bred fine bird dog like your two. I wish I could get him some time in the field and let him just run and run and exercise his true nature. I think it must be hell not to do the things you're born to do."

Linden "Like us?"

Hooker "I'm not sure what we were put here to do, but it probably wasn't to sit in an office all day and scrape and hustle to get a few things that we don't need and aren't sure why we would want in the first place. I can sit in the back yard and play my banjo and sip a glass of merlot and be as happy as a man has a right to be."

Linden "Well, you do need a banjo, don't you? And you need something that will allow you to get one and then…"

Hooker "My favorite banjo is homemade."

Linden "Okay. My favorite guitar cost sixteen hundred dollars back when you could buy a new car for three thousand. But I know what you mean. I have far more fun and get far more satisfaction from playing guitar with my friends than I ever did playing before a sell-out crowd on the coffee house circuit or a full bar. That was just for money and fame. When I play with you and Cliff, I play for myself. It's kind of like what you're doing this year over at Shindai. Taking a year to do what you want. How's that going?"

Hooker "Great! I'm happy."

Linden "You know, Dennis, I can't think of two people who are more diametrically opposed in their opinions of the spiritual side of Aikido than you and me. I wonder if you would mind telling me how you got so wrapped up in the breathing and meditation techniques you use?"

Hooker "I thank Sensei for that. You see, I had been diagnosed with Myasthemia Gravis while in the army and had been up and down with it for years. It seemed to get worse and then better, but each time I experienced an episode it cost me more than I could bear. Sensei helped me develop a program based on breathing that eventually allowed me to live a normal life. Or what passes for one."

Linden "I understand the cycle of breathing that we normally relate to Aikido. I have, over the last few years, made some serious modifications to it based on experiments in human performance that have been conducted by sports and exercise physiologists. Breathing is very important. I am not sure that it is relevant to a conversation about spirituality, however."

Hooker "You think not? Listen, Dan, there have been times that I've been subject to what other people would classify as religious experience while breathing. This is my truth. You might think that it's nonsense, but a person can't deny knowledge."

Linden "If you say it's so, I have to accept your belief in it. At least I have to accept that you believe it. There have been things that I have experienced that some people describe as mystical. I don't. I have experienced phenomena that others only dream about. I don't deny experiencing these phenomena; I just don't interpret them as a transcendental or mystical moment."

Hooker "That's something that only you can deal with for yourself. I have my own experience. For example, when I breathe I am bound by the *mokoto no kokyu* to the universe. This true breath is an echo of the expansion and contraction of all existence. I understand that the true breath not only refers to the act of breathing but also refers to the pulse of the Universe. We are bound to this just like the tides are bound to the pull of the moon and the seasons to the turn of the earth around the sun. When I breathe all existence begins to shake and my mind and heart open to new vistas, feelings, and experience. Dan, I know that you are in tune with this. I've trained with you for thirty years and know your heart."

Linden "I am in tune with the Earth, Dennis, but not because of oxygen intoxication. I am in tune with the tides because I lived by them for so long and feel the pulse of the sea even when I am not near it. I am in tune with the seasons because I have bound myself to the earth through hunting, pottery, gardening, and growing and nurturing the place where I live. I am bound to the seasons because I practice Aikido out of doors every day of the year. I love the weather, stare for hours at clouds and can sense an approaching front before the dogs can."

Hooker "Can't you see that all of these good things in your life are the result of your thirty plus years of Aikido and Aikido breathing? You started doing it when you were really just a kid. You've been doing it so long you can't even distinguish between *mokoto no kokyu* and what passes for normal breathing in some not as trained as you."

Linden "I think the same can be said for you."

Hooker "But the difference is that I train this continuously and intentionally. I need power, the power of *ki*, tangible. I need it just to breathe sometimes. I need it to tie my shoes and walk. M.G. has taken away so much of my ability to function normally that without the internal force of this higher power I could not even exist as I do. Over years I learned to live in harmony with myself, to quit battling every moment. I learned to accept the limitations of my body. My body learned to accept the limitations of my mind. Once I recognized all this conflict in myself I was able to unite my mind and body to work for the mutual benefit of my entire being."

Linden "You know, Dennis, I'm sorry, but I've never gotten that. I have never been able to see myself or anyone else as anything but completely unified as inseparable body, soul, and spirit. I just can't seem to accept the idea that you can have any of the three not totally integrated and bound inexorably to the others. Even to the extent that speaking of one or another of the three by itself is not possible. I'm not sure how they ever got separated in the first place. Clearly it was an attempt by early religions to control the actions of their members by promising rewards in heaven for the spirit that the church could not offer to the body on earth. You separate consciousness from the physical body – which you can't rationally do – and then you have eternal carrots. The flock just goes forward like the proverbial mule walking after that carrot on the end of the stick. So I don't accept any notions that there can be conflict between the mind and the body."

Hooker "I think you are making this a lot simpler than it is and making assumptions that are not very well grounded. First of all, there have been burial practices that pre-date modern history by tens of thousands of years. The idea of an afterlife for the spirit is ancient. That fact alone implies that ancient man believed in a duality of mind and body. And this was long before any organized church ever bought into the notion of the sacrament. I have a sense of that duality and to me it is as real as any observable fact that you might care to examine."

Linden "We can see a body that is damaged; where the brain has been hurt and consciousness is gone. People in vegetative states exist all over, in nursing homes and in hospitals. I have never seen a mind in need of a body."

Hooker "You are looking at one right now. My body gave out. M.G. took my ability to function. I was on welfare, Dan. I don't think I ever told you that. The welfare system took over after I collapsed while working at the packinghouse. My body refused to move one day and I endangered some people. So we were on welfare and the G.I. bill offered me the opportunity to go to college and pay some bills at the same time. I went to school, sometimes in a wheel chair. Thank God for my wife, she helped me get out of bed some days, helped me get dressed, tied my shoes. I was a wreck, but I got through."

Linden "I remember the G.I. Bill, Dennis. I remember that it paid one hundred seventy-five dollars a month."

Hooker "Well, I did get a small bit more than that for marriage and children allowance, but not much. I don't want you to think it was ever anything more than poverty, but with God and Connie's help, we made it."

Linden "That was in 1978, the year you moved to Chicago?

Hooker "Well, yes. Sensei had been coming to Chicago to teach seminars and we had met and talked a good bit. He was real interested in my problem and wrote me many letters and even flew to Terra Haute to visit me. He put together the program that I have followed all these years to try and help me lead a normal life. I had been driving to Chicago all that time and training with Takahashi Sensei, and then Shigero Suzuki Sensei, who had been sent to run the dojo.. I moved up there when I got my first job after graduating. I could finally earn a decent living without having to labor manually. Then the next year we moved to Pensacola."

Linden "Hey, that's right. I hear they're planning your twenty-fifth anniversary party."

Hooker "Your *dojo* in Denver, the Rocky Mountain Aikikai, has been going twenty-five years, too, hasn't it?"

Linden "You know, I believe you are right, however I haven't been back there in over twenty years."

Hooker "It happens."

Linden "What did Baker Sensei use to say? 'I have over twenty-five black belt students and not one of them would walk across the street to spit on my leg if it was on fire', something like that."

Hooker "Yeah. I remember him saying that. I told him I would."

Linden "I think I did, too. He was a great teacher. I miss him."

Hooker "Well if you believed in the spirit you would know that he is still here with us."

Linden "I believe that his teaching is still here with us. And that as long as I remember him and we bring up his name and talk about him, that he is still here with us. I believe that as long as his children carry forward and his line extends on this earth that he is still in a sense with us. But I don't believe that his spirit, in a somehow not-quite-corporeal essence is floating around and smirking as I trip on my *hakama*."

Hooker "I don't think it's necessary to believe in ghosts to believe in spiritual essence. My spirit is as real to me as yours must be to you. My spirit is freed when I breathe and sometimes I feel myself rising above and beyond my body. Do you get that? Actually rising away from my body. Now that is real. When I meditate I can raise my quality of life. Health and happiness are intertwined and cannot be separated. People in poor health are not happy. By releasing myself from stress and worry, I become happier and as I regain the joy in my life I become healthier."

Linden "I'm glad it works for you, but I've known an awful lot of perfectly healthy people who were just miserable."

Hooker "But that is because they don't pursue the way of spiritual harmony. O'Sensei has made it very plain that this path is highly personal and necessary for humanity. It doesn't have to be Aikido, but if a person is devoid of spirituality in his life then his existence has no meaning other than continuity. To continue living for no purpose other than finding pleasure, or just to keep on living for no apparent reason at all does not fulfill our basic nature. Our true existence is spiritual.

We are spiritual beings and our purpose in life is to raise ourselves up to the highest standard we can."

Linden "I believe that we are highly evolved beings. I believe a spirit that flows through the universe binds us to each other. I believe that we are ethically and morally bound. But, by god, I don't believe that we are any more individual in spirit than any other mammal that walks the earth. To believe that we are somehow bound by promise or obligation to a god to enlighten ourselves…well, I don't know about that. I would accept that it might make us happier. I might accept that it might make us more peaceful."

Hooker "I am at peace. I am happy. I've struggled my whole life for this."

Linden "Dennis, you're old. I'm old. We are getting even older. That is what happens to people. If you spend your life in a worthy cause, and find rewards, fulfillment, and accomplishment, you get happy and find peace. Oh, and that business with lowered testosterone, that helps, too. I know I'm more peaceful. And everybody always tells me how much more mellow I've become."

Hooker "Thank God, for that. Try applying a little of that mellowness here. The breathing practices that I trained for all those years have been described at length in my book, **Poppy's Book**. Someday I might publish it. I don't know, I wrote it for my grandchildren and it is quite personal."

Linden "I've read it."

Hooker "That's right. Anyway, the thing that is important to me is not that you agree with me, but that you understand that I live my beliefs. My heart and spirit follow these training methods and exist only because I followed them. I truly believe that I would have died years ago if I had not done this breathing and meditating. You treat this lightly, but these breathing techniques have been practiced by warriors for centuries and did not come to me lightly. I live my life with my spirit leading the way. My existence is bound inexorably with yours and my family's and all of mankind."

Linden "Actually, Dennis, I don't take these things lightly at all. I don't take anything concerning my closest friends, my family, or Aikido lightly. In fact, it is the intense seriousness with which I do take these things that causes me to make light of them whenever I can. Lord Byron once said, 'And if I laugh at any mortal thing, 'tis that I may not weep.' I read that when I was fourteen years old and have never gotten very far from it. My students are looking for something when they come here to me. My wife was seeking something when we met. When you and I met we were both looking for something. We found it in each other, my wife in me, I in her, and my students in this dojo.

"I take this very seriously. When I became your friend, that meant something to me. I would do anything, whatever it would take, for you and yours. My commitment to my students is complete. I will abide by the commitments I have made to my friends and family and students. You know me, Dennis. You know how serious I am when the glove is dropped. I believe in friendship. I believe in the given word and the implied promise."

Hooker "Just so that you understand that to me the spiritual aspect of aikido is as vital and real as breath itself. And I hope you also realize that I don't consider any part of this to be religious. I am a Christian and a lay minister and this has always caused some of my people to wonder at length about me. My use of the breathing techniques gives me a connection with my higher self, and that union also connects me to the spiritual aspect of the universe. This does not conflict in any way with my Christian beliefs. I understand scientifically exactly what happens when I breathe and meditate. This in itself does not preclude a mystical experience."

Linden "I understand the breathing apparatus and what the breathing procedure does to the body; how changes in oxygen levels alter the body's ability to process information, perception, muscle response, etcetera. I also understand that the acidity levels in the blood caused by excess carbon dioxide are registered in the brain and how these affect the breathing apparatus in terms of depth and rapidity. But are you aware of studies done recently connecting the act of breathing with the fear and flight response?"

Hooker "No, I haven't heard of those."

Linden "They were done by exercise physiologists concerned with excess adrenalin in the system. It seems that the harder we exercise the more prone we are to take in breath through the mouth. It's a larger airway and it seems natural to do this. The problem is this, the act of opening the mouth to breathe causes a response from the adrenal glands. These react to the increased need for oxygen and accelerated heartbeat. The response is a vicious circle. As we breathe faster through the mouth the body secretes more and more adrenalin. This by itself causes the heart to beat faster and the lungs to attempt to deal with the buildup of carbon dioxide and the need for more oxygen. It increases the speed that we build up lactic acid. So as we pant with exertion, we are actually causing an increase in metabolism that feeds on itself."

Hooker "Well, that's about what I expect. It makes sense. That is why we breathe through the nose in all these exercises except when we utilize *kotodama* and release breath through the mouth."

Linden "The researchers had some tennis players breathe through the nose exclusively and others breathe through their mouth. Over several months they discovered that unilaterally the nose breathers had greater stamina and lowered heart rate and respiration. They attempted to duplicate the experiments with other forms of physical exertion and the same results applied. Lately I have been trying to get the dojo students to use nose breathing exclusively in training. It seems important, for some reason, that breath be expelled through the nose as well as taken in."

Hooker "If a person uses breath correctly, that is, makes use of deep breathing, there should not be panting in the first place. No great athlete, martial artist, gymnast, whatever stands at the end of the event gasping for air. People who master their art also by default, master breathing – you can't do one without the other.

"When Sensei taught me these techniques he was trying to save my life. These were not meant to bring me to mastership. They were meant to heal a terribly weak and broken body. That they have allowed me to go further than I ever dreamed I could is not just a miracle, it is a blessing. Monks and warriors throughout the years have used these ancient breathing techniques. They are proven in many ways and over many centuries."

Linden "You know, my only reason for rebelling against the Japanese approach to this is because it seems to be one more aspect we don't need. I don't have a problem with breathing technology. I don't have a problem with meditation. I have a problem with those who insist that the Japanese method is the only one and all other approaches are flawed. But you know me. I have this resistance in many things. If you tell me that the only way to shoot a gun is to hold it with one hand out sideways, I'll be out there gripping it with two and shooting the lights out just to prove you wrong."

Hooker "Yeah, no one ever called you stubborn. Or contrary. Not twice anyway."

Linden "It has more to do with de-mystifying Aikido than it does with any problem I have with any given culture or method. In my early years I had teachers who made their students feel stupid and uncultured because we didn't know what they were talking about when they randomly threw out Japanese terms. I believe, in retrospect, that they were weak-minded fools, shodans or nidans who didn't have a clue and used mysticism and bull to hide the fact. It is easy to hide behind a Japanese term, give a simplistic explanation and then glare with disdain at some beginner student who asks a question for clarification. Too many Aikido teachers do this. This is why I have tried to explain everything with simple American terms and explanations based on scientific knowledge. You do the same, but your spiritualism and mysticism are entwined in scientific thought and you allow your students to come to you. You don't try and impress them with nonsense. Actually, I believe that we are in complete agreement with each other. As long as we don't start explaining any part of Aikido to anyone else."

Hooker "Well, I have the way I see it and you have your way. The only difference is that I do it right and you do it wrong. Actually, it isn't that you do it wrong, it's that you don't do it at all."

Linden "Is that right? Sort of the way you don't catch fish? Or shoot trap?"

Hooker "No, I'd say it's more the way you don't fix cars."

Linden "Now don't make me bring up the banjo. You don't want that. I don't want to hurt you now…"

Hooker "Like you'd know good banjo playing if you fell down and landed in Taj Majal's lap."

Linden "Yeah, tune it up and let's play. You ready for this?"

Hooker "You know, in all seriousness, I was born ready. I just thank God, Sensei and my family and friends that I'm still ready. Yeah, lead it off."

Linden "Okay, but before we play I have just one more question. If you understand the scientific explanations of the physiology of breathing, and can relate that information to the use of breathing in meditation, happiness, and health, why do you insist on calling it shijo kokyu undo and chinkan kishin and what not? Is that just your idea of making it easy on your students? Or is it something more? Or what?"

Hooker "When you put it like that I'm not sure I want to answer, however, the physical form of chinkan kishin is quite unique. My body is actually a representation of the physical and spiritual self. Sitting in *seiza* I begin to breathe in the *tanden* method. The breath is even and slow and drawn as deeply into the body as possible. My body, from the *tanden* down, feels like it is rooted in the earth and very heavy. My fingers are entwined with the index fingers touching at the tips and pointed upward like an antenna. The tips of my index fingers are level with my chin or mouth and a few inches from my face. After a few minutes of this my elbows begin to rise slightly, involuntarily. The entwined fingers expand out and upward and the upper part of my body is open without excessive tension. There is a feeling of the spirit rising to the top of my head. Sometimes I may even have the feeling of the spirit soaring outward. My will remains with my physical self, as it lives in the *tanden*. My love rises, and is brought to its rightful place. As the will to love must remain in me, the love itself must flow out to be of use. Balance has been restored. My human self and my spiritual being are in harmony."

Linden "Well then, I think we finally found our point of convergence. I don't believe that there are two separate and distinct entities named body and spirit. When I learned to pray, my minister always told me to stand up, face heaven, open my palms so that God could see that we stood before him without guile and with acceptance. We were never taught any of that kneeling, closed off stuff. After prayer we sang, and in the process of singing, or as I like to think of it, Western Kotodama, we would breathe and elevate the amount of oxygen in the lungs. If you like *chinkan kishin* so much, why didn't you just stand up and pray? Why do you feel the need to go this Japanese route?"

Hooker "I don't feel any need to go any route. If you understood *chinkan kishin* as well as you think you do, you would grasp the fact that kotodama and sound, breathing, and deep spiritual meditation aren't the same as prayer. There is a lot more to it."

Linden "And I think that if you looked at the chanting done by monks, brothers, and priests, well for that matter entire congregations, that you would realize that what you are describing is universal and that we already have a cultural equivalent to it. We call it something else, but the Japanese have no exclusive claim on human knowledge. Many Christian devotions are exclusively for the purpose of cleansing and relieving stress and joining with God's love. It is, of course, just my point of view."

Hooker "I understand these things very well. Many other religions use sounds and breathing. You told me about the trip you took to Turkey…"

Linden "That's right, the Whirling Dervishes."

Hooker "How did you come to see them?"

Linden "We were out in the Anatolian Desert, out near Capadocia. It was late, after ten P.M., and as we had been up since before dawn we were turning in. We heard a knock on the door. We were warned against bandits, you know, to be careful of people claiming to be room service or whatever, so it took a while to understand that we were being called to the lobby and were to dress and come along. Our guide had found something of interest. We drove a long way out into the desert until we came to this thousand year old caravansary. It was lit by torches and as we passed through the ancient, old stone passages we heard the most eerie music being played on drums and flutes. We came into a large stone chamber and sat and watched the traditional meditation of this sect. They simply turned and turned and turned. Music played, the torchlights flickered and the night drew cold against us. Finally in almost thundering silence we made our way back out and across the desert. It was an amazing experience. These men used breathing and motion to climb closer to God."

Hooker "Hindus and other eastern sects use sounds and breathing to achieve the same results. So do some monastic Christian orders, also the Shakers and the Quakers."

Linden "Okay. You do it your way, and I'll do it mine. When I look at your black belt students and then look at mine I would have to say we're both doing something right. It really is a privilege to be a part of a society as strong and proficient as the Aikido community. When we attend the seminars and shihan training and I always feel that the Aikido world has achieved a milestone in its growth. Being able to be a part of this group of powerful and talented individuals is really an amazing thing and I never take it for granted. The differences in all of us…the wide variety in technique and even in the application of principles…well it is something, something amazing."

Hooker "Isn't that the beauty of O'Sensei's system? He allows us all to do what our personalities dictate as long as we are true to the principles. And even though it might be hard to list out and define the principle that we experience, at least for some, it is the application of those same principles that binds us together."

Linden "Even when it comes to re-defining them. Okay, now let's play."

The Dialogs

Chapter 6

On Timing

> *"What is this magic we call blending? Time, I think. It is about time…"*
> Osawa Sensei, Boulder Colorado, 1978

Timing is critical. It is also one of the truly magical things we do. It is the essence of what makes a thing work. It is the juice, the pizzazz. It is the shot of bourbon in the boilermaker. It is the tuxedo and sequined gowns in the magic show. It is turkey at Thanksgiving, presents under the tree at Christmas, colored eggs on the lawn at Easter, and fireworks on the Fourth of July. It is cold, crisp autumn air when you head out to the football game. It is what makes the fishing work at all as the trout rises to the fly; timing is what puts you in contact with all the elements at just the right time.

I remember fishing in the streams of Northern Michigan in the late sixties. When trout fishermen, dry fly fishermen, have a chance encounter on a stream they often ask, "What are they biting on?" I asked this of a couple guys who were passing me on a stream in northern Michigan. They showed me. I didn't have anything like it in my fly book and like trout fishermen often do, they gave me one. I tied it on and cast thirty feet to the edge of the brook where an undercut bank made a likely haven for a brown trout. A trout ripped out, hit the fly, turned and disappeared. I belatedly tried to set the hook and the whole fly-fishing line assembly - leader, line and fly - came sailing over my head out of the water. The fellow who had given me the fly turned to his companion as he started to head downstream, and said quietly, "Lightning-like reflexes, eh?"

Timing is everything. Timing is the perfect pause in a great story. Timing is that sense of backbeat in a great song. Timing is knowing when to leave Mount St. Helens and head for Seattle. Timing is setting a hook, squeezing a trigger, stealing a kiss, ducking, tackling, leaving, arriving, and knowing just when to get to the airport.

In Aikido we can perfect our understanding of the joining at the nexus. We can perfect our technical expertise. We can write a treatise on keeping the nexus in the center and how we move our hips to achieve this. But if all of this is not executed with perfect timing it is all for nothing. You'll get clobbered.

Nick asked me a question after class one day about timing. I thought it over for a few days and asked him to stay after class one night to discuss it with me. He replied that he had to get home – that Lisa was waiting for him with the baby. I looked at him and smiled. He hesitated and looked back at me and nodded his head. He understood.

Nick was born in Damascus, Syria. He has a different take on life than anyone I know. A few years ago my wife and I went on expedition to the Himalayan

Mountains in Nepal. The trek was almost two hundred miles of rugged clay and rock paths that head straight up and straight down, with hardly a place to stand that is level. We traveled the old trekker's route that was supposed to prepare you for the rigors of assaulting Mt. Everest, but in truth just exhausts you, burns you down and ages your joints before their time. It was wonderful. Just prior to that expedition Nick pulled me aside and told me this. "Sensei, you're going to a very hard part of the world. They don't have electricity, radios, television, telephones or any wheeled vehicles. The roads all end where your journey begins. If something happens, if you get in trouble or hurt, try and get a message to me. Somehow, any way you can, if you do... I will come for you and get you out."

I was quite touched by his offer and the realization that he meant it completely. He would and could. Nick is a very serious man and a fine *Aikidoka*.

Nick "Sensei, you say that timing is everything. How do we practice timing?"

Linden "Most practice is done off the mat. Almost everyone does something very common that requires exact timing in order to execute correctly. Driving a car. I remember when I was learning to drive a car, my sister let me practice with her and took wicked enjoyment from her ability to do something better than me. I still remember the first corner I ever turned. I remember it clearly because I hit the curb with the rear tire. My timing was way off, you see. I had never done it before and consequently was terrible when it came time to slow and turn and accelerate.

Driving a car requires incredibly exact timing skills. So you practice each time you get behind the wheel."

Nick "How do we practice on the mat?"

Linden "Timing is really what we have traditionally called blending. All the blending exercises are really designed to get you to time your movements with that of *uke*. I guess the accumulation of actual training time doing *randori* and the exercises that are part of blending are the path to mastering timing. I think one more aspect is necessary, however."

Nick "What is that, Sensei?"

Linden "Understanding that you are actually training timing. Simply put, awareness of the process. The knowledge of what you are doing. This awareness is important so that you don't waste your time thinking about where you are putting your feet or hands or worrying about whether the technique might have worked or not. Success here is not measured by whether the outcome was viewed as successful by anyone else – only that the timing was correct. This is very difficult for most people to do. Timing is what keeps the speed bag bouncing, the ball dribbling and the guitar player picking. You need to train timing and speed just like you train *tenkan*, or *kotegaeshi* or *ikkyo*. Remember how sometimes I will have the dojo practice a technique like *shomenuchi ikkyo* or *munetsuki kote gaeshi* as fast as possible? We don't emphasize any aspect of the technique except speed. We focus on moving through the capture as fast as possible. Sometimes we alter the timing so that the attacker comes very quickly one time and then intentionally alters the speed of the attack the next. These things are some of the ways we can train speed or train timing in the dojo. Other ways are working on the bag, *shinai randori,* and simple kicking and punching exercises "

Nick "We have specific training methods for this?"

Linden "Absolutely. It's also important to remember that we have techniques to help us time an attacker's movements. Because the timing and blending process is so very important to a successful encounter we often train movements and *ki* extension exercises that precipitate an *uke's* attack. We initiate the encounter. If a person is standing, looking for an opening, getting ready to attack, we sometimes extend a look, a thrust of ki, a finger, a hesitant expectation, or energy toward the attacker and this causes him to burst forward and believe that he is maintaining the initiative. His belief that he is initiating the attack allows us to move almost before he does. Actually, and in fact, before he does. Because we have the knowledge of biomechanics and the intuition of highly trained *ki* extension, we can anticipate the attack. Knowing that it is coming we leverage ourselves into the best possible place and control the attack by initiating it, albeit clandestinely."

Nick "Doesn't that make us the aggressor or make us liable for any damages, or guilty of battery or assault?"

Linden "To the outside observer we did nothing but move when the attack happened. We disappeared almost magically and then the attacker fell to the ground hopefully writhing around in pain, that 'one strike – one kill', thing. You know, I've actually met karateka and others who believe that they can knock a man unconscious with one punch or one kick. They train at it and believe it when a teacher tells them that. I guess it could work sometimes, if the moment was perfect and all the stars in the universe were lined up just right and you were holding your mouth correctly."

Nick "You don't believe that you can overpower an attacker with one punch or kick or technique?"

Linden "I believe that you can discourage someone with one technique or a perfectly delivered *atemi* to the head. But I don't believe that anyone could stop me with one punch or kick, no matter how perfect or perfectly timed. Have you ever watched a boxing match? These are the most powerful hitters in the world. Forget all the karate, if karate was so powerful, why do all the matches end in judges decisions? Boxers hit harder and deliver more pounds of energy per square inch than anyone on the planet. And we both have seen boxers get hit with these powerful, unbelievable punches, and get back up or not even fall – just keep fighting."

Nick "Yes, Sensei. But they are wearing gloves."

Linden "Nico, the gloves protect the boxer's hands not the other guy's head. Trust me, when someone's blood is up, when he's really jazzed, a punch or even a *kokyunage* won't stop him, just slow him down. Remember Muhammad Ali? He fought an amazing fight against Joe Frazier, one of the hardest hitters of all time. Ali fought most of it with a broken jaw. And he kept getting hit on that same broken jaw. The fight went the distance and he lost on decision. You can't count on winning with one punch no matter how perfect. Hey, it's one of the reasons we learn pins. Of course, if the timing of the technique is perfect and the attacker is not aware that he is in danger – well, the results might just be a bit more extreme.

"If the timing was perfect, and I mean he never saw the technique coming, then you could do wicked damage to someone. Just remember if someone attacks you, you may find yourself fighting for your life. One technique, no matter how well performed, may not end the fight. In fact it probably won't, unless the individual who is attacking you is not serious; or unless you use one of the killing techniques. *Jujinage* and *iriminage* are killing techniques and should be understood to be such."

Nick "I've never quite been able to reconcile that idea with what we're taught about the way of spiritual harmony."

Linden "I know. Aikido is a powerful martial art that teaches even its beginning students many techniques that are designed for the express purpose of killing and maiming the attacker. *Iriminage* is a good example. We just can't mitigate the effects of a broken neck on someone, especially if we throw them to the ground a fraction of a second after breaking it. I've known individuals who believed they could temper the effects of technique and thereby control the damage to an attacker; and with some techniques I guess this is true. However there are some techniques that are killers, plain and simple.

"You need to understand that the overall strategy of Aikido is to build a better world and a more peaceful society through strength and awareness. The specifics of this are really pretty violent, sometimes. O'Sensei was not a pacifist. He was a martial art master first, an enlightened man, certainly, but there was no pacifism in his overall strategy. Or rather the pacifist nature of his soul was expressed in his tactics occasionally, but never in his strategy. I think if he could see what so many have done to his art, he would roll over in his grave."

Nick "Sensei, you have to quit holding back and say what you really mean for a change."

Linden "Okay, okay, quit laughing at me. I get carried away."

My neighbor interrupted us. He comes by for a beer and a chat every so often and is always welcome. He knows most of the students and puts up with the noise of slamming bodies, weapons cracking and hands slapping mats.

Linden "Richard, we've been talking about timing in Aikido. I've been telling Nick that I think most people, even Aikido students, practice more off the mat in everyday life than they do on the mat. Take your bird hunting for instance. When the birds are flushed, they come blasting up out of the brush flying in all directions. How do you know when to shoot?"

Richard "I wait until I've chosen a single bird and then calculate speed and trajectory. Then I point the shotgun in front of the bird to where I project it will be by the time that the shot has left the barrel and flown the distance to where it will hit the quail. It's simple."

Nick "Easy for you to say!"

Linden "No, Nick, it is easy. Once you've done it a few hundred or a few thousand times you get the knack of the timing. You figure out how to lead the bird over the end of the barrel and when to allow for a sudden shift. You get it, and it's just like when you do your first perfect *kokyunage,* when *uke's* feet slide out from under him and he flies. Just like that."

Richard "Now I want you to understand that I don't think about all that stuff when the birds break. My heart comes up in my throat, my adrenalin pounds through my chest, I jump and start to shake and then all that stuff I said just starts to happen on its own. I don't think about it at all. I've done it so many times it's just second nature, by now. If I had to stop and think about it each time, I'd never shoot anything."

Nick "I think that's probably how most people feel when they are being intimidated or attacked, heart slamming in their chests, adrenalin pumping. Is this why we train, too? So we can respond despite what our body does? Or is the training to get us to use these fears and responses?"

Linden "Training does both. It does teach us to respond with pre-programmed moves and shifts and responses, yes, certainly. I believe it also allows us to respond through all that fight or flight response to fear and aggression. In other words we train to use the adrenalin. They say it is possible that O'Sensei had actual control of his adrenal glands. The supposition is that he could call on the adrenal response when he chose, not just when he was afraid or under stress. That would make someone extremely formidable."

Nick "It would probably make you quicker, too. Make everything speed up?"

Linden "See Nick, that is exactly what I'm talking about. You know how the brain works, right? The brain moves along at the speed we need, not the speed of potential."

Nick "The speed of potential? Do you mean that the body doesn't limit speed, or that it does?"

Linden "What I'm talking about is that the brain adjusts itself to the speed of incoming data. Most of us do very little to tax the brain and make it speed up but there is one thing most of us do. We drive. The brain can handle data much, much faster than we normally ask it to handle. Think of speed-readers and how quickly they can digest and store information. But mostly think of driving.

"How many times have you driven down the highway and gone up onto the turnpike and the next thing you know you're barreling down the highway in a fast moving pack at eighty-five miles per hour? We thought we were moving along well while we were back on the highway, but turnpike speeds overwhelm that. Now after two or three hours on the turnpike we get off and move down the highway again at fifty-five miles per hour. What does it feel like?

"Doesn't it seem like we can get out and check the tire pressure and just walk along beside the car? I mean doesn't it seem like we are just crawling along? That's because the brain has adjusted to the increased level of data input and hasn't yet slowed down. Once we pull into the gas station, get a drink, gas the car and head back down the highway we are back to normal and fifty-five feels fast again."

Nick "Well…"

Linden "Okay, for some of us it does. The point is that the brain can handle much faster data than it normally does. Another good example, you might be aware that my folks are blind…?"

Nick "Yes, Sensei, I know."

Linden "My mom and stepfather are both long time users of the Federal Talking Book program from the Library of Congress. The program provides talking book machines and recordings of books and magazines to people who cannot read ordinary paper books. Not just the blind, but people who are amputees and what not. It started out as a record player and big heavy boxes with long playing records. Then in the seventies it switched to cassette and then to CD. Now, for all I know they can just go online and download MP3 files directly to their computers and use speech recognition software for rendition. I'm not sure, I haven't kept up.

"The reason I'm bringing this up is that about twenty years ago they came out with technology that would allow the recording to speed up, but avoid the chipmunk problem."

Richard "You mean how the faster you play something the higher the voice sounds?"

Linden "Exactly. They came out with some technology that would allow the voice to retain its normal timber and range, but it could be speeded up to really fast speeds."

Nick "Probably digital sampling. You could easily do it with that."

Richard "You're right. I've seen guitar effects that allow you to change the key you play in and do it in real time by just setting it into the parameters of the machine."

Linden "Something like that. Anyway, one day I stopped home and my stepfather was getting ready to listen to a new book. I don't remember what it was, but he asked me if I wanted to listen to it with him, and I did. The men and women who read for the Library of

Congress are the best in the world, really fantastic, and it's a pleasure to listen to them when you get the chance.

"My mom said dinner would be ready in a couple hours so we settled down and he started the recording. What I didn't know was that he had the controller in his hand and every minute or so he increased the speed a couple words a minute. Normally we speak at about a hundred-fifty words a minute. This is about where he started it. After two hours we were up to about four hundred words a minute and I didn't even realize it until my mom came in and said, 'Dddddiiiiiiiiiinnnnnnnnnnneeeeeerrrrrrrrr iiiiisssssss rrrrreeeeeaaaaddddyyyyyy'.

"It was as if she was talking in the slowest speech imaginable and I didn't get it at first until Russell started laughing. He had done this to people before and it actually was pretty funny. He has a pretty quirky sense of humor. The brain had upped its ability to take in data and when she came in and started speaking normally she sounded like she was on a forty-five RPM record being played at thirty-three, if you remember how that worked. Once I figured it out, almost instantly, she was back to normal and I couldn't understand a word coming out of the speakers. It was just a flying blur of speech sounds, completely incomprehensible.

"The brain is able to speed itself up to accommodate an increased flow of data. Okay, so if we take this as a granted, how do we get it to allow us to speed it up at will, in case we are attacked and need to use this faster response to help us adjust our timing?

This is the question. How do we tap the speed of potential in our minds?"

Nick "Could it be as simple as just practicing?"

Linden "Well, Nick, funny you should put it that way. It isn't as simple as just practicing, but almost. We need to practice fast. We need to push the envelope to a higher level. We need to get guys of the same rank moving at the extreme high end of their speed potential and then take guys who are much faster to push the slower ones. It goes back to what I said an hour ago. We need to be conscious of what we are doing and train with awareness that we are specifically training for speed and timing.

"Remember when we trained the boxing techniques for those few months last year? Remember how you guys felt when we returned to *shomenuchi* and *yokomenuchi* and *munetsuki*? After dealing with fast jab and right cross and left hook combinations those *yokomenuchi* felt like you could stop, adjust your *hakama*, wipe off your foreheads and then deal with it. Right? Okay, wasn't that training for speed and timing? Didn't everyone increase his ability to time technique as a result of the boxing training? Okay, follow me here. What have I done? I've equated timing to speed haven't I? I don't mean that they are the same thing. Not even close. But they are related the same way that triangulation is related to the feet. They are bound and married together. Timing trains speed, speed trains timing. Let's take a break and go into this a bit more."

Nick and I walked up to the house as Richard went home to his wife's call. We went through the back door. The air conditioning seemed icy cold after the heat and humidity of the steaming Florida summer evening. We went through the dining room and settled into the living room in front of the now cold, empty fireplace. I got us a drink and Nick asked if there were more to timing than just speed.

Linden "You know, most of the sports world's greatest accomplishments are due to speed. Think of how much we do in the world of athletics, games, sports, and even the arts that is really all about the celebration of those who have reached for and achieved top speed. Obviously runners and horse racers and car drivers are about who is the fastest. But think about the boxers we talked about. Who can hit fastest? Who can duck and block fastest? Who can ski downhill, ride a toboggan, ice skate, roller skate, run through a defensive line, dribble and race down court and then crossover dribble fastest? Who can throw five kicks in a single second? Who can respond so quickly that when an attack is launched they move smoothly and effortlessly and take *uke* down without seeming to move at all? The fastest, that's who. If you are able to respond a fraction of a second faster than someone else it begins to seem like the other person is moving in slow motion.

"Imagine being just a fraction of a second quicker than anyone else. No matter what they did, you would be able to respond. No matter how they parried or thrust or back peddled you would be able to counter their moves. No matter how they tried to surprise you, you would be able to make it seem like you were already there and waiting for them. Does this sound like anyone we know?"

Nick "You, Sensei."

Linden "Well, thanks for that, but myself and a number of others. Now couple that speed with a perfect ability to control the nexus, center, *uke* and *nage's* triangulation and break points as well as an extremely high development of *ki*... well, I think you have an Aikido master. Timing is about speed training and speed training is necessary to developing great timing or blending. Is it everything? No. But it is to developing great timing what hips are to centering or feet are to triangulation."

Nick "I thought timing was about feeling an attacker's *ki* and responding in the same instant that he attacks? Ever since I started training almost fifteen years ago, everything I've read about blending was mostly centered around *ki*."

Linden "Would it be easier for you if I said that all timing was about was training to feel an opponent's *ki*? His intent?"

Nick "I'm just saying what I've read."

Linden "You know, I want you to understand something. When I started Aikido the shodan instructor told us to extend *ki*, to feel the attacker's *ki*, to use *ki* for this and that. I have only felt *ki* a couple times in my life. Still, I think I am lucky at that. I experience it in the contact I make with other people when I train, through their extension. But, I have to touch their body to contact it. I doubt one *Aikidoka* in a hundred has actually experienced *ki* flow purely as an energy experience without being in physical contact with the other individual. So if it is this rare you need some real solid training to fall back on if it doesn't work. Train hard enough and eventually people will see how fast you are and you can tell them it's *ki*. And who knows, maybe by then it will be. I guess it's like the old joke."

Nick "Okay, Sensei, tell me the joke."

Linden "Harry looks up to the sky and says 'God, please let me win the lottery. It's all I ask. I prayed three weeks ago and I didn't win. I prayed two weeks ago and I didn't win and I prayed last week and I didn't win. Please let me win the lottery this week.' God's voice comes out of the heavens and says, 'Harry, help me out. Buy a ticket.' See, the training is like that. You have to do what is necessary, the work, and if you do, maybe you win the prize and develop some ki along the way. But you have to do the work. All of it, there are no shortcuts for this. Woody Allen says that eighty percent of success is showing up. And you have been showing up for a lot of years. Hope for the best, train for the worst."

Nick "I really enjoy training here. Over the years I've made some good friends and have learned a lot."

Linden "Ah, Nick, thank you for being here...."

Nick "Sensei, if it's not too much trouble, can you tell me exactly how you got started in Aikido? We talk about it often, how each of us found this dojo, but no one knows how you happened to get involved with this art."

Linden "It happened in 1971. I was in college at Northern Illinois University in Dekalb, Illinois. For what ever reason I had gotten deathly ill; they never really found out what the problem was, but it had caused me to spend a few days in the hospital and go through one exploratory surgery. I'm still not sure why

I was so down although I had never really felt good again after returning from Viet Nam. Anyway, I was sitting in the student union one afternoon drinking a cup of coffee when a woman I knew from one of my philosophy classes sat down next to me. Her name was Carmen and she was quite beautiful. I probably had a crush on her, but at the time had no ability to act on such feelings.

"She was in at least one and probably more classes with me. There were not that many philosophy majors at the school. Anyway, she sat and said, 'Dan, you look like hell.' I told her that I'd just gotten out of the hospital and wasn't feeling well, you know, all that stuff, I probably was looking for a little sympathy when she said, 'Dan, you just need some exercise.'

"She then proceeded to tell me all about this wonderful martial art that she practiced in the school wrestling room and all about the main school in Chicago. I hadn't really been doing anything in the way of exercise and although I had practiced judo when I was younger and had boxed in the Golden Gloves, I had not even thought about martial arts in the years since. My experience in Viet Nam and afterward left me with no desire to fight over anything at all, but in truth I was pretty attracted by the philosophy she espoused; and by her, in all truth, as well. She told me that they were putting on a demonstration that evening in the school's main field house and that I should come and watch.

"I'm really not sure why I did go. Maybe I wanted to get to know Carmen better or maybe I really felt that I needed something more in my life just then. All I do know is that I went into that room and sat down and watched. There were a number of students wearing white uniforms with white belts. I was trying to figure out what they were doing as they started stretching and moving about doing *tai sabaki* exercises. After a few minutes two men entered wearing these long flowing black skirts and after they bowed and stepped onto the mat they got on their knees and seemed to just fly all over the place on their knees.

"Nick, that was my first satori. Then, right there in that smelly wrestling room. I saw them gliding over the mat on their knees in their *hakama* and remembered that, yeah, this is what I am supposed to be doing with my life. It never occurred to me to question where that came from. What it was, it was more like a memory of what I should be doing. Can you understand that kind of experience? To see something for the first time and feel as though you remember it? That's what happened. I didn't bother to stay and watch the demonstration. I got up and picked up a flyer on the way out and the next day drove into Chicago to buy a *gi* and *hakama*. The following night I started practicing. That's pretty much it.

"I could tell you how hard it was for me, because everything in my experience wanted the art to work and you know that for anyone under about *nidan* it really doesn't. I could tell you how foolish my instructor was, in retrospect. He was only a *shodan*, but really was too full of himself and comported himself as this great master. In Viet Nam I had been on maneuvers with elements of a R.O.K (Republic of Korea) Marine Recon Company and I knew what real martial arts were about. Those guys would set up perimeters, set watches, and then set up a training area and start full contact karate practice in sixty pounds of combat gear. So Aikido training under that teacher was somewhat weak and underwhelming although I knew Aikido had great potential. Still, understand that until I met Tohei Sensei I was pretty impressed by most *shodans*, but quickly realized that they were only beginners."

Nick "Who was that teacher, Sensei?"

Linden "It was over thirty years ago, Nick. It doesn't matter anymore. Actually if he had treated me a little better I would have probably quit this art a few decades ago, but he was so rude, arrogant, and just plain mean spirited that I was damned if I'd quit. I believed I stayed my first couple years just to spite him. By then I had been around and realized that he was a mere shodan and didn't know any better than to act as he did. But it still served the purpose of keeping me on the mat until I was entrenched. Oh, what am I saying? This art had me at my first look.

"When I needed to, I could always go into Chicago and train there with the big boys. That's what I did after I left college and before I came south to Florida. But that's over thirty years ago. I think the real story is why I'm still doing it after so long."

Nick "And why is that, Sensei?"

Linden "Well, obviously it's the money, adulation, and fame."

Nick "Really, Sensei. Why?"

Linden "I don't know, Nick. I just don't know. I think I have struggled with the mysteries for so long it's become a habit. I'm not done, yet. Maybe that's all. I still have somewhere to go. Or maybe the simple truth is that the timing is not right for me to be done with this. It was being in the right place at the right time that brought me here. It was standing at a bulletin board in Chicago and seeing an announcement of a winter camp that led me to research this and decide then and there that I wanted to go to Florida and train. What great timing was that? How great was the timing that found me sitting on a chair in that kitchen playing the guitar when everyone walked in?"

Nick "When was that?"

Linden "It was during the first winter camp in Sarasota, back about thirty years ago. I was camping in John's yard there at Cardinal Mooney High School. I picked up my guitar and started playing one evening after class was over and Sensei and the whole gang walked in. Someone asked for Alice's Restaurant. It was a song, a talking blues that was about twenty minutes long and I don't think he really thought anyone actually knew the whole damn thing. I did. And by the end, with everyone singing the chorus, and the timing perfect, well I can tell you, I knew I had found my true family.

"Now that was timing."

The Dialogs

Chapter 7

On Technique

> *Technique is fine, but to be a master...eh?*
> *Transcending technique is fine, but to be a player...?*
> *You must master technique until you perform with just your heart.*
> C. Schwartz,
> Cirque de Soleil,
> Master Guitarist

Technique is the distillation of human physiology and motion dynamics geared toward breaking an opponent's center of balance. We can talk about orthopedic medicine, physiology, yoga, sports medicine and biology ad nauseam, but the truth is simple; the human body only moves so many different ways. Arms bend just so. Legs extend and contract. Hips shift. Weight transfers forward and aft. The forearm pronates and supinates.

The techniques in Aikido are not unique to Aikido. What makes the movements of Aikido unique is the way they are applied. The movements themselves – what we call technique – are common throughout the world in every discipline from dance to lion hunting. Tennis players pronate and supinate their forearms with a skill only rivaled by the best Aikidoka. Basketball players can shift their center of gravity and glide in and around each other as well as any Shihan. The Masai, lion hunters from Africa, have amazing skill with spear and staff; indeed they hunt and kill adult male lions without the benefit of firearms, using only the spear. The adult male lion is the most dangerous predator on earth. Except man. The Masai understand the limitations of their tools. The NBA all-stars know how high and how fast. Golfers intrinsically understand the loading and release properties of their clubs and how the correct shift of hips and follow-through of the swing brings the maximum of power to the stroke.

The same motions can be shown to be an intrinsic part of the Aikido techniques. The way the golfer moves his hips in the power swing is identical to the final throw of *irimi nage*. The tennis player's backhand shot can easily be visualized as a *kokyu nage*. Most martial arts have grappling and ground work that uses motions that are very much like the common Aikido technique.

Where Aikido techniques differ from all these other motions is slight. The slam-dunk – from underneath, on a reverse, backhanded, is an amazing physical movement. To watch Tiger hammer one down the ninth fairway is, as well. To see a forearm shot off a low drop by Andre Agassi is to understand *irimi*. The NFL running back probably knows more intrinsically about extension than most good Aikido teachers.

So what? It comes back to accepting the reality that Aikido is not magic. What we do is learn about the possibilities. To steal a line from the X-Files we "open ourselves to extreme possibilities". We study human physiology. We understand the limitations of the body.

We come to terms with the limitations and use these limitations as weapons against opponents.

I'll say that again. While every other sport or physical endeavor is interested in maximizing the human body – using it to its utmost – we are learning the limits of the body and then exceeding that limit. We take an arm to where it will not bend anymore, and go further. It either breaks or our partner must send his body in the corresponding direction. We bend a person's back until he cannot stand upright anymore. He either falls on his butt or his head. His choice.

We were watching the summer rains one afternoon, waiting to leave the dojo after class. The sky had just opened up, thunder rumbled and the tin roof over our heads rattled and clanged from the downpour. The rustle of bamboo leaning against the side of the building added to the clamor. Overhead, trees swayed in the storm winds and lightning flashed bright in the dark gray sky. It was just a typical Sunday afternoon in Florida. While we waited I asked two shodan candidates, Chris and Erik, to show me some techniques against a choke grab from the rear. They jumped up, and began to attack each other.

I let this go a while and then asked them to stop, catch their breath, and then proceed, but to use none of the techniques that they had previously used.

Chris "I don't think I know any more. I was already kind of reaching when I stopped just then."
Linden "What about you, Erik? Do you think you can find any more?"
Erik "I can try. I'm willing to give it a try, at least."

Linden "Okay, but Chris go first. You know, this is a lot like improvisation in music, sometimes. When I play guitar with my friend Kane Lamberty we might noodle around in a song for twenty minutes or so looking for something new to happen. We keep trying and looking for a melody shift or a chord that fits some new way. Kane says you sometimes have to play everything that you know before something new can happen. It can be like that. So now you've done everything you know. Let something new and fresh come forward. Dig around. Try. You can hit a lot of sour notes that don't fit anywhere except in some weird jazz format when you dig. But you can't find something new unless you try. That's why we're here; one of the reasons, anyway."

Erik moved to get behind Chris. He reached out and grabbed his *gi,* his training uniform, by the collar and swung around to get a grip from the rear. As he attacked, Chris did what he had done already several times and dropped his shoulder a bit and reversed so that his elbow rose and smashed into Erik's face. At the last moment Erik took *ukemi* and avoided the blow by dropping to the mat and rolling away.

Linden "Chris, you've already done that a few times. Why don't you relax and let him take a grip. You already know you can break him before he gets there. Explore a bit, hey?"
Chris "Yes, Sensei."

This time Erik came up fast and hit him harder with the choke than he was expecting and he faltered forward, almost falling. He began to struggle with Erik's hands, his wrists, his arms – he was getting nowhere fast and I called out "*mate*", wait.

Linden "Chris, relax! You are in a pretty good position if you think about it. Both his hands are tied up. Okay, they are around your throat, but they aren't in a position to protect Erik, are they? And he might have you by the throat, but he doesn't have your feet, legs, torso, hands, arms, elbows, or head, does he? No! How about this, just bow forward from the waist and lower yourself to your knees at the same time. Go ahead!"

He did this and Erik flew over the top of him propelled by the force of his momentum. He let go of Chris' throat and slammed the mat with his now-free hand to ease the force of the break-fall. As Chris stood up I saw he was smiling slightly as Erik attacked again. This time he allowed Erik to come into place and as he was taking the chokehold Chris *tenkaned*, turned back, and then reversed again. Erik found himself loaded up on Chris' back once again and had to release and slam his own hand into the mat to ease his fall. Again. Now Chris was definitely smiling. Erik flew at him and disappeared under him as Chris allowed him to enter and then turned with a classic *irimi*, entering technique. I let them play a while and then as Chris started to repeat moves called a halt before I let Chris attack Erik.

Linden "You see the importance of studying technique, don't you?"

Erik "Sensei, you are always talking about the fact that after you get to a point of mastership, you don't need technique. Is it like a road map of where we are heading? Or is it actually the road? Like the path we need to walk down to reach mastership is paved with technique?"

Linden "No, only good intentions. Actually it is more like an analogy for language than a road. Think of technique as the alphabet. We learn the alphabet as children and the constructions of words, words into sentences and so on until we have a language.

"If we were to decide to study the concept of Shintoism and wanted to truly understand, we might learn Japanese. After many years of study we get to a point where we can speak, read and write Japanese, but we don't yet really know anything about Shintoism. However we could now take up the study in earnest, because with real understanding of the language comes real understanding of the concepts and principles.

"It's the same as a child who decides at age four that he wants to be a doctor like his daddy. He has to learn to read and write his native language for many years before he is capable of understanding the textbooks written about medicine. This is what technique is to the study of Aikido.

"We learn technique for about ten years or so. *Sandan* level is really about knowing more than the basic technique. You must have developed a great deal of understanding about timing, center, ki, and what not, but sandan level is primarily the point where it's acknowledged that you are in command of all the basic technique. You are a master of the art by then, but there are many levels of master.

"Now we can start teaching you advanced Aikido. You need to be conversant with all aspects of the basic technique before we have a common ground with which to discuss the principles that are the heart and soul of what we know as Aikido. Technique is the language. By using the language we can now learn the principles. Aikido is the discipline behind the principles. Without the language it is impossible to discuss the principles or to get to Aikido. Erik, go ahead."

Erik walked to the center of the *dojo*, the training hall, and stood as if he were listening to the rain pounding on the tin roof fifteen feet over his head. Bamboo rustled in the thicket and thunder sounded in the distance. Chris walked to him slowly and moved behind him. He grabbed him in a two-handed choke. Erik stood there. Chris waited. Erik seemed to concentrate on the rain sounds and was drifting along until Chris pulled him closer and then Erik dropped his hand gently and reached for Chris' testicles. Chris pulled away abruptly while still holding onto Erik's throat and Erik reached up and took Chris by the wrist as he bowed forward. Chris slammed forward over Erik's back and landed hard before he had the opportunity to prepare. He hit very hard, yet Erik had done little and moved easily. Chris got up slowly and moved in for another attack.

Erik now seemed slightly out of focus, almost vulnerable, yet each time Chris moved in Erik responded with a different subtle counter until Chris stepped back and said, "You have no openings." He shook his head and continued, "There just isn't anywhere to attack."

Linden "Chris, that was excellent. Understanding that experience is a great point in your education. Realizing that Erik was oblivious to your best intentions is a great moment in your understanding. Erik, well done."

Erik "Thank you, Sensei. I just tried to let myself see the opportunities that Chris was showing me. After a moment he seemed to have more vulnerabilities than threats."

Linden "That's because you have studied techniques carefully, remember them, and see so many different possibilities that you don't get hung up on particulars. Remember however, just knowing techniques doesn't mean you can execute them. The pillars of technique are timing, center, triangulation, break point, the nexus, and *ki*."

Chris "So technique is the same as Aikido? You always say that Aikido is the perfect understanding of all of that plus technique. What am I missing?"

Linden "Damn those slippery words, anyway. Listen, each of the eight pillars supports the other seven. Each one is dependant upon mastery of the other seven. Technique by itself isn't enough. Neither is timing or any of the others. This art is a cosmology."

The rain had left absolute humidity. Temperatures hovering around eighty-five found us thinking about air-conditioning and a cold drink. I asked them and another student, Bill, if they would like to join me for some refreshment in the house and they all agreed. It is rare that I ask students in. It is important to maintain a separation between home and work. However, these men have been training with me for years, have helped during construction projects and been a close part of my family. Asking them in is like asking family to dinner.

We sat in the cool air conditioning and admired some fine work done by the masters at Coors Brewery. My wife was gone for the afternoon so we put on a video from class of Erik, Chris, Cliff and Luke doing *shomenuchi ikkyo* through *shomenuchi yonkyo* in *suwariwaza*. They had been training for their *shodan* test for about nine months and were rounding into form, but I wanted to look closely at their technique and video is a perfect way to point out inconsistencies and anomalies.

Chris "Sensei, I like technique. I feel solid doing it and doing things carefully, the same way each time. Why do you always say that once you reach mastership there is no technique?"

Linden "Why do you think?"

Chris "I'm not sure. Is it because of the inconsistency of the attacks – so you can't really set up a technique, or aren't sure what you will do? Maybe you have no use for technique. That is, you can beat an opponent by atemi, or timing."

Linden "Chris, how do you define technique?"

Chris "I think a technique is a set move that can be repeated each time, designed to break a person's balance."

Erik "Or break his wrist!"

Chris "Well, yes. Sure it could break a wrist, but I think for a definition that breaking balance is good."

Linden "Sort of like a left hook. Or, maybe a crossover dribble. It's a set move that can be repeated in a given circumstance that will result in foreseeable results. Okay, I like that. But I wonder, what if it doesn't produce the same results. What if you weren't sure what would happen? How would that figure into your definition?"

Chris "I'm not sure, but I think I would hesitate to use something that I didn't know would work."

Linden "How do you know that any of these techniques will work?"

Chris "Well, we practice them. We do them over and over and if we do them correctly, they seem to work each time. Take *kotegaeshi*, if *uke* doesn't take the fall, his wrist breaks. Maybe his arm breaks if he doesn't fall. So you know if you do it right it will work."

Linden "What if it doesn't?"

Chris "But it does."

Linden "I'd like to believe you, Chris. I really would, because I want to believe. I'm sort of like that X-Files guy, Mulder. I really want to believe. But, see, I've tried to do *kotegaeshi* against attacks by some pretty tough guys and it didn't work. I remember training with Charlie from Baltimore at *Shihan* training. Charlie's wrist doesn't bend for anyone unless he wants his wrist to bend. He is probably the strongest Aikidoka in the world. I remember a guy thirty years ago from Chicago, Frank Knapp. No one could budge him with it.

"There is a man in Germany named Andrew Wilby, a sensei who has been training over thirty years who is unmovable. He has a rock for a center. I think most folks would have had a tough time moving Kevin Sparkman Sensei or several others I can think of. So if there are folks out there who can beat a technique, how can you trust it? How can you know it will work?"

Chris "Yeah, but Sensei, nothing is perfect. There's always going to be someone who you aren't going to be able to beat with a single technique. I probably couldn't throw you if you didn't let me. Well, I mean, I'm sure I couldn't."

Linden "Then what good is it?"

Chris "Well, it works most of the time."

Linden "If someone is willing to be a good *uke*?"

Chris "No, almost all the time. I know the difference if someone is just falling for me or if I actually broke his balance."

Linden "Do you?"

Chris "Yes. If Erik is just going through the motions, I know it. And when I break his balance we both know it. You can feel it. You can tell the way someone moves if they just take *ukemi* or if you forced them into it."

Linden "Okay. You've convinced me. But I am a little unclear about what you are going to do when it doesn't work. What do you think of your technique when it hangs you out there with nowhere to go? When the guy you are trying to overcome with finesse is picking you up...wait. I've got a good example.

"My Dad hadn't seen me in a few years when I was living out in Denver. I came home to visit once over Christmas. He was living on the St. Johns River up near Lake George. We were having a beer and talking about what I was doing out West; for a living, for fun, you know how that kind of talk goes. We were sitting on the couch and there was this coffee table in front of it, you know what I mean, a standard oblong table.

Anyway, we got around to the fact that I had been promoted to *nidan* in Aikido and had started a school out there called the Rocky Mountain Aikikai. It's still there, by the way.

"My Dad wanted to see something of this Aikido he'd heard me talk so much about. Let me just say here that we are German and Irish by descent so there had probably been some drinking happening by then. I got up and went around to the front of the table and my Dad stood up on the other side of the table and I told him to grab me. He reached over and grabbed me by the lapel of my shirt and I slowly put him into a *nikkyo*. You know how painful this is. I didn't want to hurt him, so I did it slow, but when I had gotten to the point that I knew it really had to hurt he still hadn't flinched.

"Now my father was a big man and strong as hell, but this was too much for me. I nailed him hard with the *nikkyo* and he finally reacted. He lifted me up with the arm I was mangling and turned and threw me into the wall over the couch. I slid down the wall and he bent over and lifted me up again by both lapels and gave me a big bear hug and said, 'God damn, it's good to see you, boy! You should come home more often!' I wasn't able to do much except hug him back and have another beer. My mom is still mad at us for scaring her half to death.

"So much for my *nikkyo*..."

Chris "But you didn't want to hurt your father, did you? I mean, it was just for fun, for showing off. If you had been grabbed by someone like him you could have made it work, right?"

Linden "I don't think so Chris. There are men out there that are tough, impervious to pain, willing to take whatever you can give rather than break off, slack off, or stop their attack. Chris, listen to me. Technique is a tool that we utilize to learn Aikido. It is the alphabet that we use to write our story about how we perceive the real world. It is the palate we paint upon to create an image of the limits of human endurance. It is the sum of all our knowledge of human physiology, human endurance, pain, balance, strength, and power. But it is not the be-all and end-all of martial art knowledge.

"Police departments send their people to classes where they learn things like *nikkyo*. They practice doing it to each other for an hour. Now tell me, even if they remember it – do they know *nikkyo*?"

Chris "Probably not."

Linden "Why not?"

Chris "Because they can't really do it. They'd be like a white belt that learns to walk through the technique, but can't apply it in a real-time, real-life situation. They don't understand the principles that make it all work."

Linden "Okay, now we're getting somewhere. So to go back to your definition of technique – that it is a set move that can be repeated with a foreseeable result of breaking a person's balance – is it the move that breaks the person's balance? Even if it is done by a white belt or a cop? Or is it something else that breaks the balance? Obviously if the move is the thing to be feared, anyone could learn and practice it, right? But without the context of the rest of the aspects that an *Aikidoka* brings to technique it is shallow, empty and insignificant. Technique is not Aikido. Technique is how we learn Aikido."

Bill "Sensei, I'm sorry to interrupt, but..."

Linden "That's all right Bill, go ahead."

Bill "Well, about the police or the white belts that train and go through the motions, it seems to me that they only do the technique with their arms and hands and wrists. Good *Aikidoka* do it with their whole bodies and use all the principles that you've been talking about."

Linden "Bill, that is a terrific observation. Really great. You are what, a fourth *kyu*? I would hope my *nidan*s would have gotten that. But even that, it isn't the end of it. It is not the end, but rather the beginning. It is the place where we start. Once we master these movements we are about third degree black belt, *sandan*. That means we have trained in all aspects of Aikido for about ten years. We are getting there. The completion of the technical training coincides with the maturation of many different areas of the student's training. That is why *sandan* is such an important rank. This is the beginning of wisdom. We are now at a point where we no longer have to spend our time dealing with the process, but rather the actual fact of doing. Triangulation deals with how we place our feet to keep everything in our best possible place – inside our triangle. Center is about how we move our hips to keep the nexus in the best and strongest possible place. The eyes constantly update us as to the availability of *uke's* break points. Technique gives us a wealth of possibilities to choose from in the decision making process as we join and begin leading *uke* to his break point. Timing is the actual process of joining with uke at the nexus. And ki is the spiritual strength we draw upon to allow us to overcome an attacker despite greater size and power.

"The culmination of these things is Aikido. These are the steps to mastering the art. Once a student is a *sandan* we can start teaching him these aspects of the training. We have a common vocabulary. Think of it like a student who goes to high school and then college. One would assume he knows something, but then he gets accepted into med school and it is there – built on the foundation of chemistry and physics and anatomy that he learned as an undergraduate - that he begins the study of real medicine."

Erik "But what are you doing? We are practicing to test for *shodan*, not *sandan*. Shouldn't we be working on technique instead of spending all the time we do on these other things you say we can't understand? Or that we aren't ready for?"

Linden "Good question. I guess this is my experiment. To see if I can get you to realize the full potential faster than we normally think is possible. Why do you think I limited the Dojo enrollment to people with Masters degrees there for a couple years? Why do you think I pick about one out of maybe ten to actually join the group? I'm cheating! I'm picking and choosing my students because I want to take the best candidates available. I want to see if I can lead you guys to mastership faster than we normally think possible. Not in twenty years – but ten! About the time most of us understand this art we are too old to get anything done, but if we can cut ten years off the training time - well, that would be something great. If I can get you guys there, maybe you can pass it on to your students, and they theirs.

"I consider this my own personal challenge."

Chris "But it still starts out with technique, doesn't it?"

Linden "Of course it does. That is the root of the language. Technique is the foundation. It is the first one of the eight pillars of Aikido wisdom. Go get **Seven Pillars of Wisdom** by T.E. Lawrence. Read it and you will understand why I have co-opted the title like this."

Teachers like Andrew Wilby and Ayan Kaya are the future of Aikido in Europe and Asia. Here they are studying the eight principles of mastership.

The Dialogs

Chapter 8

On Triangulation in Aikido

This is the chapter I have received more emails and letters about than any other. And in truth it is an incomplete chapter because my editor and close associates have all warned me not to print my conclusions about the significance of true triangulation in regard to the secrets of the mathematical universe. Before I pass on to the main text let me give everyone a path to explore on your own. Go Google the term 'golden triangle'. You will find references to drug smuggling and growing regions and all sorts of other blather, but what you are looking for is the mathematical equation that transforms the triangle into the vortex or spiral. I got caught up in photographing Aikido technique and superimposing the equation over the photographs. What I discovered is that the same exact spiral vortex (and the descent there-from) is the identical form of the universe. Galaxies, hurricanes, all the great spiral powers can be defined by the equation known as the golden triangle. And Aikido is right there. It is mathematically provable. That's too much hocus pocus for my editorial staff, so it has been excluded from this book. Don't be lazy. Go look it up for yourself. Good luck, and don't spread it around. If you must spread it around, at least mention where you got it from.

There are a number of different concepts that converge in the act of doing Aikido. It is difficult to break them down into their unique characteristics, but it is essential if we are truly to understand what mastership involves. Basic triangulation involves the way we stand in front of uke, the way we position our body when he attacks, and the way we maintain the nexus while leading him to his break point.

One of my senior students asked me why other senseis don't talk about this at all. My response was that they probably do, but in different terms. Most use obscure Japanese phrases that over time have come to represent these ideas to them. They don't bother to translate because they know that it takes many years of hard training to internalize these concepts and often discussing them gives a false sense of accomplishment to those listening.

My feeling is that you get exposed to ideas all the time. The ones you are ready to internalize you embrace. The others are stored away and remembered in those moments we describe as *satori*, the sudden understanding. I try to expose all students to this knowledge knowing that when the time comes, they will embrace and internalize it. The more they are exposed to it, the more certain that it will be available when the right moment comes. I may not be there. I may be long pushing up daisies, or just out for a beer. But knowledge truly is power. I want all my students to be prepared for their life long journey toward mastership.

The other thing that is necessary to understand is that Aikido is a huge endeavor. Most senseis specialize. This is normal and understandable. When I attended the University of Illinois my major was philosophy. One of my professors taught the ancient classics, Plato and Aristotle. One taught phenomenology. One taught Berkley and Hume. One specialized in the Germans, Kant in particular. All were full professors. All taught philosophy. None had a damn thing in common with the others academically. This is normal and Aikido teachers are exactly the same. There was little in common between Saito Sensei and *Doshu* Kisshomaru except that they both taught Aikido.

Triangulation is my term for what some refer to as position or posture although it does not actually relate to these in any specific sense. In brief terms, triangulation is where we place our feet and how we control uke through controlling where he puts his feet. Simplistic? Yes. Easy? No. Actually it is much like the rest of Aikido, the more you know... the harder it gets.

Mike, one of my teaching assistants, and Clifford, a *shodan* candidate were helping build a deck onto the back of my house. We needed a place for students to relax after class and a place for my wife and me to spend the cool winter evenings out of doors.

Mike "Sensei, I've been trying to use triangulation to help me work better when I do hard physical projects. Are the ideas behind what we do in Aikido and how we work interchangeable?"

Linden "I believe so. When I worked for a commercial firm we used to have to maintain our vehicles ourselves. Sometimes the lug nuts on the trucks would not break loose and when that happened the men always brought me in because I would go out and sit on my knees and take the lug wrench and turn them off. To them it apparently looked effortless and I often caught them trying to do it themselves sitting on their knees. As if that were the trick. What I really did was simply to place myself directly in front of the troublesome nut and arrange the wrench so that the sides were equidistant and then I would forget about the wrench and simply turn my body. I think it is the same for the great arm wrestlers. They lock the arm – sort of the way O'Sensei used to claim he could crush green bamboo under his arm – and then turn the body. It's just one technique, really, not even interesting except as an example of how what we learn on the mat translates into real life."

Clifford "I don't know how this relates, but if I don't hold my guitar in a particular spot and angle, my speed and technique suffer quite a bit, eh?"

Linden "As if any of us could tell. But yes, I can see that."

Clifford "Mike mentioned triangulation. When did you first hear that expression? Or did you adapt it in order to explain the Japanese words for it?"

Linden "It is like anything else in Aikido, definitions can be very slippery. Just about the time you think you have something nailed down it becomes something else and exceptions to the rule are everywhere. When we use Japanese terms we are able to deny the pre-conceived idea that would be associated with an equivalent English term. A good example is *kotegaeshi*. In Japanese this means something like a wrist twist or throw. However if you don't know that, you learn the archetypal form of the technique and call it *kotegaeshi*. Wrist twist isn't articulated or written and so you don't have a preconceived idea that what you are doing is supposed to be twisting someone's wrist. Obviously, if you know the term and technique you realize that twisting the wrist is the least of the parts of this throw. By leaving the English out you never confuse the issue. You associate the technique and the new name, and they become one and the same.

"Everyone seems to get the impression that I want to change Aikido from Japanese terms to English terms and that just isn't true. I want to keep the names of the techniques in Japanese for the previously stated reason. It's the names of the principles, and the means of identifying the basic principles that I have chosen to Westernize."

Mike "So with technique then, the Japanese name is like a new tool. You have to learn how to use it and discover the limits and potential. If you think it's a hammer, you're going to just use it like a hammer. We need to call it something else."

Linden "Exactly. *Ikkyo* is another example. It means first technique. That's all. However, once you learn the archetypal form, the principle of the technique, *ikkyo,* takes on a complete new meaning. By saying *ikkyo* instead of first form we put no association to the form other than the principle itself. And it becomes *ikkyo* in our mind.

"Okay, so the ideas that are expressed as technique can be defined almost completely by example and step by step demonstration. The ideas that I define in English terms are far more slippery. The notions of the break point or center or triangulation need, I think, more explanation and definition. I don't think it behooves us to try and obfuscate in order not to confuse. These ideas are worth defining. The Japanese terms are too archaic and steeped in too much history, culture, and mystery to do us, as Americans, much good. Unless you really enjoy pretending you are some mystical master. And there are those out there that do enjoy that. Of course, there are Americans out there that teach Aikido with a Japalish accent too, who have never stepped foot in Japan. That's another topic, all by itself."

Clifford "So by defining a term, you think that we are less likely to understand what it means? I'm not sure I get that."

Linden "Just the opposite. The important thing is that the name can define itself and take on a life of its own. So we need to be careful how we use words when we teach these concepts. Trying to describe triangulation in Japanese terms is like trying to teach someone how to rebuild an engine by speaking to him in a foreign language. Maybe by using your hands and pointing and miming certain motions you can get through it, but man, is that hard! Wouldn't it be easier to speak English and just get it done? That's why I use these terms instead. I care about you understanding and learning. I don't really care about all the trappings of being a sensei, with the bowing and 'S

Clifford "We really appreciate that."

Linden "And I think that someday, when you really understand what I'm saying, you will. That is why I've made the effort. Now let's get to this.

"Triangulation is the term I use to describe the power position in Aikido. Both uke and nage benefit from this. It is also the position which generates the most effective distance and closing in the combative moments of an encounter."

Clifford "I thought that Aikido was not supposed to be combat. I thought that it was the resolution of conflict – the idea of no fighting. If we don't fight we move with the attacker and resolve the problem, eh?"

Linden "Then how do you describe watching O'Sensei rush up to an attacker and smack him to the mat before he can even get his *bokken* up to attack? No Cliff, we talk about a lot of things that came from O'Sensei and were misinterpreted as non-violence. All these spiritual, and mystical, and 'the universe is love' notions are really the efforts of a very old man to unify his life's work and beliefs. He was in search of spiritual realization and he was a master fighter and genuine tough guy. In his last years he tried to unify his life's work, Aikido, with his religious beliefs. And he did it. He created something unique. He created a police art.

"Aikido is a police art, not a martial art. All one needs to understand this it to look at what a military is and what it does. A military kills people and destroys things. Is that what we do in Aikido? No, of course not. Just the opposite. O'Sensei said that 'to foster and protect all life is our mission and prayer'. What does that sound like? Ever see a police car with the words 'To Serve and Protect' on the side? Think about it. We don't learn to kill, we learn to protect. I think it would be wonderful to re-define and create a new category for Aikido and call it the first and most powerful police art. It would certainly change a lot of misconceptions about it and help clear up a lot of samurai fantasies.

Mike "Can we talk about the notion of violence and pacifism or even the idea of aikido being a police art some other time? I want to understand this better."

Linden "Of course. Now let's look at the stance and relationship of stances that are the fundamental core of Aikido. For years we called the basic notion of a stance '*hanmi.*' There were only two, really, left and right. The relationship between *uke* and *nage* was either '*ai*' or '*gyaku*' *hanmi* meaning either we stood with our feet as mirrors or the reverse." I grabbed a piece of paper and drew this diagram. "This is *gyaku hanmi.*"

I took another piece of paper and drew another diagram, one that anyone with two weeks of Aikido experience would easily recognize.

"This is *ai hanmi*. You see the feet are harmonious. They blend and fit together like two people dancing. This is the traditional description of the major stances. As you well know the stances are dynamic and change depending on the attack that is being used, whether a punch, grab or kick.

"If you look at the position that *nage* maintains while being attacked you will notice that besides his effort to maintain the nexus of energies in his center – we've already discussed this – he needs to maintain a consciousness of his posture and position that is best described as triangulating. Let's look at his."

Mike "Sensei, we only have two feet. How do we create a triangle?"

Linden "The triangle is created by the two feet and the center. Those three points create a triangle. As we move our hips, head, feet, or shoulders we change the triangle that is our posture. As we extend the distance between our feet or flex or extend our knees we expand the triangle. Look here."

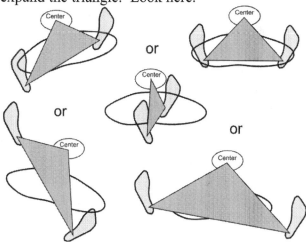

I quickly sketched five sets of feet and torso on the paper, each with a different configuration of body, feet, and center and then drew the triangles through each set. Cliff and Mike put down the screw guns they had been working with and came over to look at the diagrams and each bent down to study the paper. I showed them how the intersections of lines each time formed a triangle. I showed how as the arms are lifted from a person's side that the confluence of the two hands in front of the torso clearly defines where the center is.

Linden "You can see the differences in the stances. Some are wide and some are very narrow, but they all have a clearly defined triangle that forms as result of the placement of the feet, body and center."

Clifford "The center is the area between the hands if you relax and raise them to where they meet in front of you?"

Linden "Um, basically. It is smaller and larger, higher and lower, denser and softer and harder and every other adjective you can think of, except it can't be precisely defined. But once you experience where your power is located you know exactly where the center is. Here, take this screw gun and drive this three and a half inch screw into the floor and joist. Hold it out here to your side and just drive it in. With one hand."

I watched as Cliff tried to do this and when I heard the drill tip spinning ineffectively I stopped him. "Mike, you do it." He grinned and I watched him drill the screw tightly into the deck and handed him another. "Now do it again, with your other hand." He leaned over and shifted his weight, centering his strength in his grip and drove the next screw into the wood. "Okay Clifford, try it again, this time with both hands, and keep yourself centered over the drill."

He took up the drill and after a couple false starts, where the screws tended to skitter away, he got it started and then he proceeded to drive it all the way into the deck.

Linden   "Clifford, why was Mike able to drive it so easy and you had such a hard time?"

Clifford   "Because Mike was a carpenter for ten years?"

Linden   "Well, yeah, that's right. And he knows where his center is. He knows how to work, how to dredge up the most efficient power in the most awkward place. He had to do this over the years. Had to find out how to drive that nail or push in that screw when all the rest of his body was contorted and twisted in awkward shapes. He learned to transfer his strength to his most accessible part and make that his center. When confronted by something as simple as driving screws into a deck with either hand, you can see it was no problem. You, on the other hand, have never done this and don't know how to find the most efficient way to drive a screw into a deck so you have to experiment. If I tell you that the best way to do this is to keep it in your center, and you actually listen and pay attention, eventually you will get very good at it until you encounter an awkward situation and then you will have to experiment and feel around and try different things until you find what works. Unless of course I happen to be there and show you how to do it."

Mike "That's what you do on the mat, and here while we talk. You show us the best way to approach our center."

Linden "Sure. I'm showing you where your center is all the time. All good *sempai* do this. All the senior students who stop mediocre techniques and give the junior students a hard time are doing it. Maybe they don't realize why, but they sense that there is something not right with *kohai's* technique. It's one of the reasons that *sempai* – senior, and *kohai* – junior, relationships are so strong and important. They are always helping you find your center and helping you strengthen it.

"Now let's look at how the two feet and the center create the triangle that is so important to our understanding of the Aikido experience. Look back at the last drawing and see the positions that make up all the triangles that we create while defending against an attack. Let's see how they relate to the position of *uke* as he attacks. Come on over here." I took out my carpenter's chalk and drew on a piece of slate.

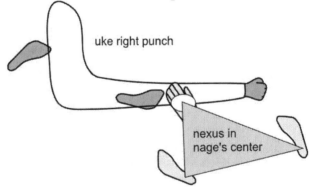

"If we take this to the next position, it's easy to see that as *nage* extends from his center he can easily break *uke*'s balance and center by leading the nexus to the break point in front of *uke*. Look."

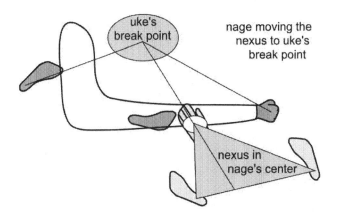

"You can see that the combination of uke's feet and the triangle of his break point unite and combine with the triangle of *nage's* feet and the nexus which leads to the break point. The point where *uke* and *nage* meet is the nexus. If we see this technique as *ikkyo*, where *uke* has punched and we have moved off-line and then extended him forward into *ikkyo* – if you look it is very easy to see – then you can see that the break point is where you lead the nexus in order to make *uke* lose his balance and fall flat on his face."

Mike "I see this because we do it so much. Baker Sensei did it exactly like this. I've never seen the triangle before now. Wow, that's amazing!"

Linden "This is why I want to share these ideas so much. You will never see this technique the same way again."

Clifford "What happens though, if you move *nage's* feet further back or over a bit. So it isn't so symmetrical?"

Linden "Okay, let's try it and see. I'm not much on drawing motion, but see if you can follow this here. If *uke* strikes, *nage* enters and establishes a nexus in his center. Then *nage* moves outside and leads *uke* to his break point."

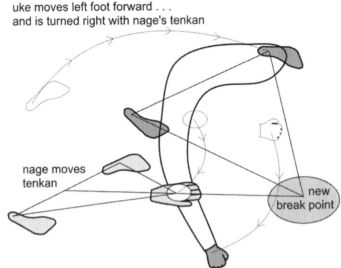

"You can see that this is *ikkyo tenkan*. If you can't then this might be too advanced for you – but that's okay, you will see it eventually. Circles and triangles are the stuff of true understanding. Once you get through the ideas that I am showing you, combine them with motion and speed and timing - that's where practice is so important - and then you are really beginning to master this art. The break point changes as the dynamics of the triangles change. See where *uke* ends up as *nage* moves in and leads him to the outside? Each step uke takes creates another opportunity for *nage*. Each step is the creation of two new break points. You see, you always have two chances to break *uke's* balance wherever he is."

Clifford "Which one do you take?"

Linden "Well, if it were me, I'd take the easier one."

Mike "How do we know which is the easiest one?"

Linden "It depends on his balance, his posture, his speed, and the second attack that is coming - you do understand that all technique is delivered to the second attack - right? Well, almost all, maybe the exception is *atemi-waza* and I could probably make a case for that. You see, if he is bending forward at the waist a bit, do we try and stand him up? Do we encourage him to stand up? No. We encourage him to keep bending – which puts weight on the balls of his feet making them hard to lift and we continue until he drops forward and we finish. If he is upright and leading with his center, in other words a pretty good martial artist, we do better to try and turn him over and reach for the rear break point. Round heels and what not. Examples are everywhere."

Mike "Why not move him up, if you can? Like in i*riminage*."

Linden "Mike, it's really an extension of his attack that raised him up. You know that. I always train to the weakest effort that works. I might be injured; might get old (Get old? Older?), I might be weak – there are a lot of reasons why you need to let the Aikido do the work and not your body. Young people want to get out there and tear it up. The reason that you see so much gray hair on Aikido mats is that the concept of Aikido is not reliant on excessive strength. You must be strong, and be able to move, but if you understand how to use the center to control the nexus, use triangulation to control the center and use the break point to control the attack, you will be able to do Aikido with just about anyone at any age and condition. Now really, could a woman who weighs one hundred pounds defend herself against a trained attacker who weighs two hundred pounds – equally trained? Of course not. That's why there are men and women's divisions in sports. That's why there are weight divisions in sports. Common sense tells you that, no matter how much people believe in their own invincibility. It's silly to think that Aikido training could allow otherwise."

Clifford "But Sensei, then why would a woman or a small man train?"

Linden "Because most really bad people don't have the discipline to train at all. And in that case, a small woman who is trained in Aikido has an enormous advantage over a non-trained attacker who merely sees her as a potential victim. She can overcome an attacker in that case, but only if she uses surprise and a very fast response. Once an attacker realizes that a woman has training he will simply use his brute strength and high pain threshold to subdue her. Of course, there is always the possibility that she will train for thirty years and become a shihan, maybe then it is different. But otherwise, take away the gender bias and the results aren't pretty. Almost any male over 4th kyu can badly hurt and humiliate women aikidoka of any rank if they choose to ignore the strict rules of aikido training. If they don't take ukemi, for example, and continue attacking, or if they attack with lightning speed and ferocity or anything other than what she wants him to do... well face it, it would be bad. I believe that is a problem. So many women actually believe they can win a fight simply because men they train with stay within the confines of training. Most women in aikido live in a false sense of accomplishment. They are actually incompetent, but believe just the opposite because someone told them they are a third or fourth degree black belt. But a black belt in what? Aikido is a very specific, very narrow and regulated system. Face it, a good example, there isn't a person on this planet who can throw me with kote gaishe unless I let them. You see? But most aikido black belts will tell you they can do it easily. They just haven't ever had anyone refuse. Kote gaishi is the easiest technique to stop, but everyone likes to take those big, stupid break falls... and I don't.

"There are always a few women who stand out of course. There are women who weight one hundred eighty pounds and can bench press their own weight, but they are as rare as Joan of Arc was humble. That is all for another discussion, however. We need to focus on the fact that if a woman did this right she would have an outrageous advantage over the typical untrained attacker.

"Here is a perfect example. A number of years ago, I'm talking about 1978 or 1979, I was working in a shop out in Denver. The foreman, Kent, was a very hard guy, hard to get along with and very rude to the workers. He was often very threatening, physically. One day he and I got into a disagreement over something, who knows about what, and he grabbed me by my lapel. He was brandishing a shop hammer in the other hand and even though I knew he was not about to hit me, I had had enough of his threats.

"Now if the truth is to be told, I might have had a small problem with authority at the time. Still this is no reason to be threatened with bodily harm with a hammer. Today that would be called aggravated assault. Anyway, he grabbed me, and as he did I took his hand in my opposite hand and nailed him to the floor with a *nikkyo*. His eyes flew open wide as saucers, his hand literally threw the hammer across the room and his knees actually bounced off the tile floor. He looked so surprised! Well, that was it. He got up, slinked away and left me alone for a week or so. Finally he came up to me one day and asked me what I had done to him. I told him that I had been studying Aikido for many years and what it was about.

"He was really interested. We began to talk about Aikido then, once in a while, and after that incident we got along much better."

Mike "I'll bet."

Linden "Wait, it gets better. One day I am at the front counter and this guy walks in and says he has a package for Kent S----- Sensei. I ask, 'Who?' He says, 'Kent S--- Sensei.' I tell him we don't have anyone in the shop named Sensei. He says that it is a title, like 'esteemed teacher'. He wants to see Kent. I was somewhat in shock, but I was recovering fast. I asked what Kent taught. He told me that Kent was the top *Tae Kwon Do* teacher in Denver, perhaps all of Colorado. Well, Kent wasn't there, but I offered to give the package to him and the young guy handed it over and then left.

"As it turned out, Kent had never wanted anyone to know that he practiced and taught *Tae Kwon Do*. No one knew. I learned a great deal from his secrecy; that sometimes it is a very wise move. He came back from lunch. I handed him his package and just stared at him. He realized that the cat was out of the bag and then we really began to talk. We actually became good friends. Our dojos trained together, had parties and it was all very good.

"But you see the amazing thing was, he was crushed by that *nikkyo*. He didn't expect it. He never saw it coming. He was this big, tough, bad guy who was hard-core, trained, and mean as snake spit; and here this guy, twenty years his junior, skinny and dumb-looking, just killed him in one-half second. It drove him crazy, so we shared secrets. This is what I mean when I say that Aikido can be deadly effective when used by just about anyone if that person uses it with stealth and does it right. It worked in this case against a very well trained attacker. Of course, I was a *nidan*, at the time.

"Are you guys clear on this? Any questions?"

Mike "Can you explain why I can drive a screw, left handed, way out from my center?" He asked this smiling.

Clifford "Or why I can play the guitar behind my back, upside down, while onstage?"

Mike "Show off."

Clifford "It's in the blood."

Linden "Okay. Okay. Mike can do that because he practiced doing it for years. Same as you, Clifford. But let me ask you a question. Can you do the same job better, faster, more precisely, more smoothly, and with far less effort if you bring it out in front of you and do it in your center? Of course you can."

Clifford "But then it wouldn't be doing Jimi Hendrix."

Linden "I know you think you've got me there, but just wait. If the technique requires you to do it behind your back or out to your side – and believe me some do – then what a master does is to expand his center to accommodate for the gap, or distance. Have you ever seen Osawa Sensei do the 'Good Morning' technique? Just like that. *Uke* attacks right up the middle. Nage *tenkans* away and opens both arms wide and *uke* runs smack into one of them.

"Now, according to my descriptions this would not be in his center. Except that nage is moving both arms equally. He expands his center to accommodate for the entire sphere of his existence. Watch..." I took the chalk and drew another diagram. This time I tried to show motion with an arrow.

"It is difficult, but as *uke* attacks, the raising of nage's arms and the extension of his conscious center creates a balance that allows for an exceptional and unusual strength. A powerful nage knows that by extending his center he can balance himself and be strong well away from his core."

Mike "You see people doing technique, *kokyunage* for example, where they extend one hand out and over to their side and even around behind them. Does this all mean that that there is no real strength in their technique?"

Linden "I think it means that they have very cooperative *ukes*. Few accomplish true mastership and those individuals who do rarely perform outside their centers. They know where their strength is. The same way Mike can be strong and focused out there in left field and you can play one hundred twenty-eighth notes behind your back. You extend your center out and it provides a balance and strength to what you do. It takes practice. In fact it is very difficult to actually do at all. The person doing these *katate-dori kokyunages* with a single hand over his side is just playing games. He couldn't make this work if he held a knife and the *uke* was attacking the knife in order to protect himself. An *uke* would break him. No, you have to keep the action on the opposite side of your butt to keep the power in the technique and to stay triangulated.

"And there is something else as well. Remember that a triangulated stance is really a pyramid for those who reach mastership in the essence of balance. We have break points in front as well as the rear. Those who master this, Osawa Sensei, Walter Payton, Michael

Jordan and the like, use all four points and understand that the pyramid is the most stable structure that can be built."

Clifford "Do you have to keep *uke*'s center away from there – that space to the opposite side of the butt – to break it?"

Linden "Boy, talk about a stretch…yes. But when *uke* attacks, he is almost always in a non-centered position. He may be focusing his center on the attack, but he is extended forward and committed to a forward movement away from his center. *Nage* is able to focus on keeping the nexus of energies in his own center and therefore is able to generate more power to send *uke* to his break point. I love this 'Aikido is the way of spiritual harmony' stuff, but if you aren't stronger and more centered than your opponent, your spirit is going to be pretty short-lived. As for that space opposite the butt, uke often ends up on his butt, so no. That is a prerogative of *nage*. Look at this diagram again. I'll show you how large *nage* can get.

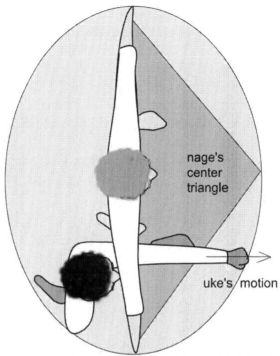

"See, *nage* is large in this position. Koichi Tohei Sensei has taught us to enlarge our centers for years. *Uke* runs smack into the extension and ends up flat on his back, right on his butt, if you will. *Nage's* center is opposite his butt; you must remember the counter balance that makes us human beings able to stand upright and what also makes us so hard to knock down. We just have to remember the basic principles of triangulation and apply them with lightning-like defensive techniques and motions, with balance, always centered, always maintaining the nexus, and we can be masters of Aikido. It's easy. Just takes a couple decades of hard work and study."

Clifford "Just like playing the guitar. The way Eric Clapton plays."

Mike "Or cutting a deal like Mike Eisner."

Linden "I knew you'd understand. Here is a simple association to help you remember this. The center is almost always reached by turning the hips toward the nexus. The nexus is reached by moving the hands and wrists toward *uke*'s attacking motion. Triangulation is achieved by moving the feet in conjunction with the center towards uke's break points. Technique is always applied in *nage*'s center, not *uke*'s center. *Ki* is extended at all times in conjunction with proper breathing. What could be simpler?

"Now go back to work, please. We have a deck to build."

The Dialogs

Chapter 9

Strategy

When we started to build a dojo in Orlando we had to rely on faith: that we could re-coup the many thousands of dollars invested, that we would find and attract promising students, that our life long goal of leading a group of students learning Aikido was possible. We did have a strategy however, and a little more than faith to base it on. A good strategy is worth a lot of trial and error.

In Aikido, which is after all a police art, the idea of strategy is rarely explored. Strategy and tactics are the very center of the eight pillars of wisdom.

Curtis, a student and sensei for Shoshin Aikido Dojo, accompanied me on a five day tour of Europe after we conducted a seminar in Frankfurt in 2003. Riding in a private automobile with Arne at the wheel and my hands clenched into white knuckled fists, we skipped across the German countryside at over one hundred miles an hour. We were driving south toward the Alps and the area of Germany known as Bavaria. It was, of course, October.

Arne "Sensei, we are coming into the region known as Bavaria. Can you see the Alps ahead?"

Linden "I see clouds on the horizon. I think."

Curtis "It's the Alps. This reminds me of coming across the Great Plains and driving from the east into Denver. You can see the mountains for a long way."

Linden "What town are we coming to, up ahead?"

Arne "It is Fussen, where the Mad King Ludwig built Schloss Neuschwanstein. We are going there."

Linden "Another castle, I presume?"

Arne "Well, ya."

Linden "I wonder, sometimes at the strategy of putting so many castles in such remote, difficult areas."

Arne "I think they are only remote if you don't live there."

Curtis "Good point."

Linden "No, I mean that while the castles are beautiful and strong, they were obviously not intended to protect the people who lived in the valleys and worked the fields – they were obviously only intended to protect the king and his cohorts. Look at this beautiful structure. It is a monument to greed, excess, domination, feudal values and inhumane treatment of serfs and taxpayers."

Curtis "Do you think Mel Brooks had it right?"

Arne "Who is Mel Brooks?"

Linden "A comedian. A filmmaker. He said 'It's good to be king!'"

We laughed and climbed up the steep hiking trails that led up the mountain and to the keep of the Mad King. The winds howled and the cold wind blew bitter but the day was clear and we had great views of the castle and the surrounding valley. Later that evening we were having dinner when Curtis asked the following:

Curtis "Sensei, do you think that the strategy of the King was to let the enemy take what he wanted from the countryside, assuming that there was little value in anything other than the serf's toil, and preserve his true wealth behind the stone walls?"

Linden "I don't really have too much understanding of the way of kings. I think that perhaps each had a strategy to maintain what he perceived to be his, to the exclusion of anyone else. Strategy is how campaigns and businesses and governments operate. Without a good overall strategy it is pretty hard to define what we are doing after all. I suppose some just went forward living each day, never giving thought to their destination or their objectives. Some, I am sure, had hard strategic objectives and managed through precise control of their tactical resources to realize these objectives."

Arne "What is the difference between a strategic objective and a tactical objective?"

Curtis "A strategy is the big picture. What we deem to be the reason for being. At IBM it is to make the best office machines and market them well. At Ford it is to build the finest car at a reasonable price. Tactics are the means to that end. IBM might choose designs that are stable and develop a marketing team to promote that idea. Ford developed the assembly line to keep costs low and production consistent. Those are tactics."

Linden "Thanks, Curtis. That was a good definition."

Arne "Sensei, do you have a strategy in your Aikido?"

Linden "Not me. I only do what I am told. I did not create Aikido or develop its purpose. That was O'Sensei. He had a strategy. In fact his strategy is what actually defines Aikido as a martial art. Our overall strategy is to do the least harm. We protect and defend all living things and do so while doing the least harm to those who cause the problem. What changes is the tactics of the situation. It is very liquid. What would be a ruthless butchering in one case can be a benign gift in another. We need to apply our own ethical imperatives toward the overall strategy, as well. Together, they weave a template of moral conscience."

Arne "How we respond, our tactics, vary as to the intent of the attacker?"

Linden "Exactly. Once you understand our strategy the tactics become crystal clear and anyone can extrapolate the right thing to do in any given situation. For example, if your brother-in-law has too much to drink and he has been fighting with your sister, and then throws a punch at you – well, you can't very well kick him in the head, knock him down, dislocate his shoulder and break his wrist, can you? That would not work in a family situation. You might even be forced to accept more pain and suffering to yourself than you would normally deem acceptable in order to not damage your sister's husband. But how much, and at what cost? And if you are capable of dealing out this kind of defense toward someone you ostensibly care about, aren't you obliged to deal with others at the same level of protection? If you aren't thinking about these things, you are not practicing Aikido."

Curtis "Can we look at this a little closer? I don't understand why I would have to suffer at all if I were defending myself against anyone, even if it was my brother or brother-in-law. Is it part of the Aikido strategy that we should suffer?"

Linden "Of course not. That is the rule of life itself. Buddhism, you know. All life is suffering. Get over it. No, we don't have to suffer to defend our own body, but sometimes we will if we do this right. Let's forget the brother-in-law for now and come back to that later. Let's take a far more extreme example.

"Say we are walking through a crowded parking lot at night and suddenly hear screams. We look up and see three men dragging a teenage girl to a waiting van. She sees us and begs us for help. We rush over and the first man steps up to us and shows a knife; he snarls something about killing us if we don't go away. Got the picture? Okay, so our first response is to protect ourselves. What's the best way to do this?"

Curtis "It would depend on how he was holding the knife. If he tried to thrust..."

Linden "No. The best way to defend ourselves would be to back up and simply go away. We could simply leave. This is where things get unclear. When O'Sensei said, 'to defend and protect all life is our mission...' did he mean for us to weigh each situation and choose the path that would protect the most life, or the most important life? If the most, then obviously the right thing to do then would be to allow the three men to leave with the girl. If they rape her or kill her it only affects the one girl. If I try to save her I might do serious harm to three individuals. Which is the right thing to do? Obviously it is to save the innocent girl at the expense of the three bad guys.

"How do I come to this conclusion? I apply my own ethical barometer to the situation and see how it fits on my morality template. In my Christian ethic, in my Judaic ethic, hell, in just about any ethic I can think of it is my responsibility to save the girl. Now the overall strategy of Aikido says to do this causing the least harm to all individuals involved, right? Okay. So if not for that, what do we do?"

Curtis "Shoot them?"

Arne "Maybe in America..."

Linden "Well, sure. I mean, if we were armed, why not? They are clearly dangerous, rapists and possible murderers. The police would give us a medal. But it is not what we have pledged our life toward. Could we shoot them and still follow our true path?"

Arne "Yes, sure. If they pulled guns instead of a knife."

Linden "Right. If the level of violence escalates to that level, then we would have to respond at that level. Actually, there is an interesting notion to consider here.

"When a police officer is confronted by someone wielding a knife he has legal permission to draw his fire arm when the attacker is about twenty-one feet away. The rule of thumb is that someone with a knife can cross twenty-one feet and cut you before you have time to clear your side arm. So if an individual armed with a knife confronts us, we need to consider the distance as well as the fact of the knife.

"Actually, I think if I had a gun I would try and stop the whole assault by bringing the gun out – the same way the attacker showed me his knife and tried to stop my interference. The threat might be enough to make them let the girl go. But we are getting sidetracked. Let's look at the situation from the initial moment we came into it.

"The attacker shows me the knife. My choice is to go away or to fight. Forget this nonsense that Aikido is not fighting, that notion is a semantic hell and I won't go there. I choose to engage the knife-wielding fiend and step forward. He thrusts. The rest is history. I take the knife, check to see that the attacker is not moving and do what?"

Arne "Go rescue the girl."

Linden "What do I do with the knife?"

Curtis "Use it. There are still two attackers, presumably armed as well."

Linden "Good call. Yes, there are two attackers and they are probably carrying knives, guns, clubs, or what have you. So then I engage the two attackers trying to push the girl into the van; move right up on them. I am willing to do what is necessary and I tell them to let the girl go. If one of them comes at me with a knife or club, I will respond at the level of defense that is necessary to protect the girl and myself. If this can be accomplished with a scare, or an *irimi nage* then fine, if it takes more, then so be it. If, at the end of it, there are two dead men and one hurt, okay, that is my level of competence and I have accomplished my goal. If there are three attackers rendered unconscious, but alive, I've done even better. If I have the personal power and Aiki skill to make the three of them stop, let the girl go and then restrain them until the police arrive, I have done the best I can. That would be true Aikido.

Do you remember the story Terry Dobson told about the coal miner on the train? Now that was fine, the highest level of Aikido strategy.

"You see, it is hard to get some people to realize and to understand that it might be perfectly all right to attack someone with a knife, and still be within the Aikido strategy. If we are protecting someone or trying to defend someone, yes, this is possible. We all aspire to the realm where we can take on six attackers who are all armed and to defeat them with open hand technique. I'll tell you guys, no one I know can do that.

"The important thing is to understand that the tactics are about situations and the focus of tactics must be on the ethical considerations of each situation. Once you begin to engage that kind of thought you automatically know that there are some things that are basic truth and some things that are mitigating influences on such truths. The way we go is the way that is pointed out in our overall strategy of doing the least harm."

We finished dinner and then took a walk through the old Bavarian city. It was nearing ten o'clock and the town was shuttered and closed for the night. Early the next day we set out across the border into Austria by going through the ancient town of Reutte and up into the Alps. I learned a great deal about the region, what constitutes an alp, an alb, and a high pasture, all the while watching in awe as we climbed higher and higher. I have been on a long, four week trek through the Himalayas and I was surprised to see that the Alps are every bit as impressive in their own way.

As we neared the pass we encountered an unexpected, early season snow which became heavier and heavier until visibility decreased to mere meters. As we crossed the highest point I asked Arne to stop the car so I could get out and play in the snow for a moment. As a Floridian, it is still a true novelty to see so much water in this unusual form. Not to mention that I loved those few moments of frigid cold, until it settled in down my back and drove me into the car.

We crossed the Austrian countryside, through a lovely valley that seemed to stretch on forever until we arrived in Liechtenstein. I was a bit surprised at the lack of borders and guards, but Arne assured me that these things were all a matter of the past. Europeans now travel from country to country the way Americans travel state to state. Interestingly, there were certain and definite differences between the countries. The differences were subtle, but if we paid attention, we could see variances in architectural detail and building design between Germany, Austria and even Liechtenstein. We visited the Count's castle (of course) and had a fine lunch of wildwurst, käse, and schwarzbrot mit trockenem wein.

The next day we were on to Switzerland and chocolates, cakes, coffee and that wonderful invention, the second breakfast. While enjoying kuchen und kaffee mit milch we watched the Swiss children climbing through the open vistas to sled across huge fields mottled green and snowy white.

Arne "Sensei, do you use strategy and/or tactics everyday?"

Linden "I think everyone does. Unless we just go stumbling around in life waiting for whatever might happen to us to happen. We plan, strategize and manipulate our lives without even realizing it. Some people are so good at this that they become quite successful at business or what have you. Some turn their skill at this to controlling dojos or other groups when they really shouldn't have that kind of authority. They just assume it and take control. Some find they have no patience for these things and turn their skill at strategy toward avoiding other people. But once again, the overall strategy of our existence determines it all. What is the purpose of existence? What is our objective? Then we apply the tactics of the moral template and use whatever means we can ethically accept to reach our objective.

"Let me tell you a story. Years ago, in Denver, I had started an Aikido group we called the Rocky Mountain Aikikai. It still exists and as far as I know is still under the fellow I left it to, Jack Ross. This event took place on the occasion of Saotome Sensei's first visit to Colorado, back in the late seventies.

"I asked Saotome Sensei to teach one class for my students only, the night prior to the seminar and he agreed. After class, it being a Thursday night, we always went out to this particular restaurant for a few drinks. The same happened that night. Let me say that this restaurant was rather nice and had big overstuffed chairs and couches in the lounge and one of those chairs was a particular favorite of mine. Needless to say, Sensei was sitting in that particular chair when I walked in. He must have either noticed my reaction to seeing him there (despite my attempt to remain completely neutral) or perhaps someone mentioned something to him. For whatever reason he made a show of insisting that I sit in my usual place. He and his wife sat to my right. We could converse easily as this was a quiet place and very comfortable.

"He asked me why so many of my students were not wearing *hakamas* and I answered that they were very expensive out West and that most people could not afford them. He seemed fine with this explanation and we went on to discuss the western way of life. He seemed fascinated by the mountains. He was intrigued by all things there are to do in the mountains and said he would like to take some time while he was there to try certain things. Of course we were thrilled at the prospect of taking Sensei skiing or fly-fishing.

"We had a few beers and some food. It was a cold blustery night and inside the bar was warm. I began to relax from the tension of bringing Sensei to the bar. He obviously liked my students, was happy with me and them and life seemed to be perfect.

"At one point he leaned forward and said that he would like to try skiing, and would he have enough money? Does it cost a great deal? Sensei and his wife were not wealthy, but it might be fun. I told him how everything was priced, the cost of equipment and lift tickets and he considered it for a moment and nodded his head. He thought that everything sounded very expensive. After a bit he asked about fly-fishing. Did most of us do it? Most nodded and agreed that they did and we went on to invite him to try it. He said that he didn't have a rod or reel and flies – any of the stuff he was sure he would need, but we all told him we had extra fishing rods and could loan him whatever he needed. We were enjoying ourselves, looking forward to taking Sensei up into the mountains and sharing all these wonderful activities.

"After a bit he leaned over and said that he thought it was wonderful that my students were so nice and so many had other sports and activities they enjoyed. He said it meant a lot to be a martial artist, but that people should enjoy all the things that life has in store. Then he said, 'Dan-san, how is it that your students can afford to spend hundreds of dollars on skiing and fly-fishing and that they can't afford to dress properly when I come all the way out here to teach them? Why can they buy extra fishing rods, but not a *hakama*? You brought me out here and your students aren't even dressed properly on the mat. Why is that?'

"My good feeling faded. The complete level of my incompetence loomed up and I was shocked into silence. I wanted to cry and merely hung my head. I turned to my highest ranking student and told him quietly that the next day everyone would have a *hakama* if someone had to fly to L.A. overnight to acquire them. He said, 'Yes, Sensei', and quietly informed the group.

"But he did not stop there. I don't remember anymore what all he had to say, but it was most unpleasant. I remember excusing myself and going outdoors and after a moment his wife came out and punched my shoulder. She said 'Congratulations.' I was absolutely crushed. I looked at her and she said it again. 'Congratulations.' Then she said, 'Sensei would only do that to someone he considered a true student. It means he has accepted you as his own. I know it hurts now, but when you realize what it means, you will be happy.'

"She was wrong, that event never made me happy. Sensei had accepted me as a true disciple and over all the years he certainly chewed me out a few other times and probably worse. But never has he led me down the primrose path and destroyed me as completely as he did that night. I didn't even see it coming. He spent three hours patiently setting me up and then dropped the hammer. He was a master of tactics and strategy."

Curtis "You wouldn't do something like that would you?"

Linden "Curtis, you are a bona fide rocket scientist. You make the space shuttle fly. You are a Ph.D. I can't believe that anything I could ever do would be subtle enough to fool you for an instant. But someone else? Yeah, I might, but I am more straight ahead than that. I have a different style. Subtlety and intrigue are the hallmarks of Japanese thought. I am more the type to just tell you right out. My strategy for running my dojo is simple. We are family. Families talk things over at dinner; they discuss important issues out front. It is almost impossible to keep secrets in a family and I maintain all my relationships with all my students out front. No one has to wonder what I think or what is going on. I tell them. Hell, I tell everybody.

"Does it cause embarrassment sometimes? Sure. But if you can't weather some embarrassment you aren't tough enough to be a martial artist in this dojo. My prejudices, my inclinations, my limitations, my successes, all are right there for everyone to judge, accept, reject, embrace, deny, or ignore. I expect everyone in my family to be equally open with me.

Would I set someone up to knock them down in front of everyone else? Probably. If I thought it would make a point or send a message home. Would I do it for meanness? No. Would I do it for fun? Maybe, if I thought it would get a laugh."

Arne "That sounds mean, Sensei."

Linden "I know. It is my greatest failing. I always look for the humor first and mostly I'm not strong enough to keep from blurting out a fast one-liner. Usually it is inappropriate, silly, or just plain stupid and I often regret it."

Curtis "Then why do you do it?"

Linden "Because I often get a laugh, too. It's the old Lord Byron thing, I guess. 'And if I laugh at any mortal thing, 'tis that I may not weep.' I like to laugh. I think it might be the best thing we humans do."

We left Switzerland and drove east to France. Once again the change was obvious when we went across the border. Where the Swiss roads were immaculate and the road shoulders manicured, neat and tidy, the French roads were pitted and weeds and debris cluttered the shoulders. We let Arne take us where he wanted. But we soon realized it was to more castles, ruins and finally to the palace at Haute Koenigsbourg. We spent that night back in Germany in the Schwarzwald, the Black Forest.

All my life I had assumed that the Schwarzwald was a large, dark, forest full of first growth trees and dark hollows. It came as somewhat of a surprise to me therefore when I discovered that it is really an area of mountains. They are rather low, on the order of the Smoky Mountains in America, but the deep dark glens more than matched my imagination and the towering trees gave a lie to the notions of 'first growth'. They have been harvesting trees here for over two thousand years and it is a tribute to the conscience of the European forester that it is still filled with fine, ancient trees.

Curtis "Sensei, tactics become necessary when we are forced to apply our overall Aikido strategy to self-defense. Doesn't this impede our ability to react?"
Linden "Yes, of course. When your brother-in-law throws that punch at you it would be far easier to hit him between the eyes and wait for him to regain consciousness than to capture the attack, guide him to the floor and pin him until he calms down. That's the point."
Curtis "The point?"
Linden "Sure. When O'Sensei charged us to modernize the world of the martial arts it was not only because the times were changing, but also because the world consciousness was changing. We are evolving as a species, one would hope. We need a new way to do things besides responding to violence with escalated violence. Just like the incident in the parking lot, the easiest way to deal with it would be to simply walk away; the easiest way to deal with your brother-in-law would be to hit the stumbling, drunken fool. The easiest way is rarely the best, anymore. It is like the evolution of a new language. Linguists say that the older a language, the simpler it becomes. The younger a language, the more complex.

"So Aikido and this new concept of doing the least harm is rather difficult to master. It is far more work and much more difficult to command. As the art ages and matures we will find easier and simpler and more efficient ways to accomplish the same thing. But this is just our bad luck now. We are already immersed in the project and must continue to push forward. Mastership is possible, but it is never going to be easy. We devote our self, our selves, to the way of Aiki and we make ourselves better human beings. This is what O'Sensei wanted for his followers. He knew that by evolving, we would help those around us evolve. He knew that by teaching we would help those who follow us teach. He taught that by loving mankind we would show those we meet every day what it is to love.

"This is our true dream. It is evolution through hard training. It is understanding that having no fear is the most important part of true happiness and fulfillment. When we fear, our hearts become suspicious and weak. When we fear, our love is small and something we give only sparingly. We train to be strong and powerful so that our love will be there for all to see and for those who would, to emulate. We must be proud. Yes, proud. We also must be humble. Not some fake, hypocrite humble, but we must really understand how much we need other human beings. Knowing that need, we understand true humility. The teacher who does not understand that his place only exists because of the students is a poor teacher at best. True humility is understanding that our place is one of service to the student. We are limited in our growth to the extent that students allow us to grow. I have always been suspect of any teacher who has not gone out and found a place to train, inspired beginners to come and raised them up from stone white belt to *sandan* all on his own. It isn't much to walk into a dojo with a half dozen advanced students and go on from there. Not much. My praise is for those *sandans* who go out and do it from scratch. They are the real warriors. And they are the ones who go on to become real masters. As they grow and mature they have the background to make wise decisions and the humility to understand that learning is always a miracle, and that we rarely have much to do with it beyond showing up.

"Perhaps it is time to see that mastership is not some elusive dream, but one that is attainable and an accepted goal. Throughout history, martial art masters have trained students to become masters and upon graduation, they were sent out to open their own schools or found their own academy. It seems only in modern Aikido is a student to stay a student for life and never be recognized for his skill and achievement by being granted 'mastership' and be released from his Shihan. I have been released and I hope that my teaching will help change that for others too, as there are many masters already and many more to come."

Curtis "Is the strategy then to harmonize your own spirit? Or do you want to make more teachers?"

Linden "We must harmonize our own spirit. People say to me, 'Sensei, how are you?' I am in harmony. I am at peace. My spirit is complete and peaceful. Each year I am more at peace and in harmony. How can I affect you? I can't. See, it is like teaching. We cannot teach, students learn only by our example. We cannot force someone to learn something. How easy that would be! If we could force someone to learn what we show, then there is no problem. But we can only lead the way by example. We have to be what we want them to see. If we try to show the way of spiritual harmony, we need to have a spirit that is in harmony. We need to show our students that we are in a state of grace. We need to be calm, strong and with great center. We need to have dignity. How can we teach the way of spiritual harmony if our spirits are upset? We can't. So it takes a great deal of time. We must work constantly. But we have a path, and that path is the study of Aiki principles. It is fostered by the study of tactics and strategy."

Curtis "So the proper strategy is focus on our own evolution to the exclusion of what takes place between two people in combat?"

Linden "Partially. But without the connection of two people, without the emotional response, there is nothing. We need to connect emotionally. We need to understand and realize that each person is unique. There is always a different direction with human beings, always a different approach. Always a way to connect that is different each time, and unique. There is never a connection that is the same as another. Each time we connect is different and each time we connect can never be repeated. Do you understand?

"So we are all still growing. We all have more to do and further to go. Our goal is to make the world a better place. It is that simple. I have a direction, to try to help *nidans* and *sandans* understand Aiki principles. That is very good. That is admirable. I know that the human connection is the most important principle. We must have love in our hearts for mankind. Not this silly stuff of 'I love you, oh, oh', but true love, warrior's love. You must have the kind of love that a man will die for, this kind of love.

"Many stories are told of great samurai who gave everything for their master and lived their lives devoted to the master's cause, never questioning, never doubting. When John and Peter and James devoted themselves to Jesus they gave everything to be his disciple. This is true love and devotion, not mere words and noise. And this is a true strategy, not just fumbling around in the dark."

Curtis "Sensei, you say your life is full and happy, but I know that life hasn't always been this way for you."

Linden "Life has been hard. Disciples often walk a difficult road. When you walk a path that is covered in stones, that is all up hill, and the weather is bad, it is hard. But you smooth the path for the next person, and you lead the way. Together we can all go farther. O'Sensei wanted the world to be a better place, so Aikido, the way of spiritual harmony, is what we do. Hell, if everything was always easy, then everyone would do it and it would have little value."

Curtis "Is it then your strategy to teach O'Sensei's principles exactly as you have learned them?"

Linden "No. As I said, times are changing. Even Doshu Sensei's world is passing away. My mission is to adapt O'Sensei's message to the modern world. The complete master of Aikido must be someone who understands the principles completely. He must have great understanding of the traditions of the past, but not be stuck there. He must be able to interpret O'Sensei's teachings so that the people he is teaching can understand them – not everyone is the same. He must be someone who is more concerned about passing on the teachings of Aikido than building his own ego and personal power. My mission is to find and teach many individuals to be complete masters of Aikido. To build teachers who can teach their own students proper respect and understanding. To build teachers who can understand the principles and who can teach the principles. I am a direct student of O'Sensei.

"Do you see that this is a direct line, unbroken from O'Sensei to me and to you? This is a great honor and a great responsibility. The more you are honored, the more responsibility you must carry. This is a burden. You must be strong and your will must be greater than your ego. If you realize that the work and responsibility of being a *shihan* is so great, and you labor constantly to deserve this honor, you will never be trapped in your own image of yourself as a master. Your ego will never grow out of control. But the way that you do this is to work so hard at giving the knowledge back to your own students that you do not have time to think about yourself.

"My students are the next generation. It is vital that these new teachers be afforded the respect that they deserve. So often the old gray beards favor only each other. We like to sit at the top of the room upon the stage. We like to bring our own throne before us as we enter, but the truth is, we are just old. That's all. The younger men and women have just as much juice, are faster, stronger, and when trained properly, are just as good. The *uke's* job is to make us look good.

"There is more work to do. The world will change more and more and we must constantly be ready to change and adapt with it. But we must be strong on the things that we know are basic. It is the way we teach.

"The techniques may vary, the style may change from teacher to teacher, but the principles do not vary. They are the rocks in the stream that we use to cross to the other side. The water rises and falls, freezes, warms or dries up. The rocks are forever."

We slowly wound our way through the Schwarzwald in the general direction of Frankfurt. I believe if we had not run out of time that Arne would have loved to make a stop in Heidelberg, home of many castles and ruins, but we were running short on time and we had to make our way back. We stopped for refreshments and as we once more got under way Arne asked me an important question.

Arne "Would you do it all again? Would you devote thirty-five years of your life to learning what you know? You have told me that it was only this spring that you were able to finally put it all together. So many years, so much time and work. Was it worth it?"

Linden "If you live your life as a warrior, you must have patience beyond passion. You decide on a strategy and then begin implementing the tactics that will bring all the forces of your world to bear on the result. It took thirty-five years for me to finally understand the principles of Aikido and now I am too old to really be much of a warrior anymore. Did I waste my time? I don't think so. I can teach these principles in a way that does not confuse and obfuscate their real meaning. I will contribute a great deal to the understanding of what Aikido really is. So in that regard, yes, it was worth it. I am too old to be much good any more, but through my understanding I will be able to teach people the true principles and in such a way that they will be able to master them at a much younger age. And that is a fine thing. If that was my purpose, I will have succeeded and then I can say it was worth it."

Curtis "When you told us the story about Denver and the *hakamas*, was that meant to describe Sensei's personality or to describe how he used a tactical assault to teach you something?"

Linden "I would not want to describe Sensei to anyone. He is a unique individual to each of his shihans and their relationship with him is their own. He was once asked how many students he has. He responded 'Each one student'. So in that sense, even if I could describe him, it would only be my observations of the way he is with me.

"So clearly then I was using the story to show how he approached a teaching situation. Merely telling me that my students should be wearing *hakamas* was insufficient because I was not smart enough to realize what he was saying. When he was asking me why they were not wearing *hakamas* for him, I did not catch that he was telling me that he considered this dojo, my dojo, to be part of his organization. He was telling me that we were accepted and a real ASU aikido school. I didn't get it from the question, so he fiddled and finessed the question so that I could get it. He is very subtle."

Arne "He asked why your students were not wearing *hakamas*. He was telling you that they should be wearing *hakamas* because your students were actually his students? What significance did wearing of *hakamas* make?"

Linden "Oh, nothing really. It is just that Sensei does not consider you to be dressed unless you wear a *hakama*. Many organizations don't allow you to wear one until you reach some advanced rank, *nikyu* or *ikkyu* or *shodan*. I know why and it's all silly, really; what difference does it make if you are a *shodan*? Sensei thinks you should wear one and he's right, it makes a big difference in your training. So his students do.

"He was telling me that we were accepted as his students by asking the question. When I didn't respond with anything but some excuse about the cost he decided to teach me a lesson about subtlety, the Japanese mind, tactics, strategy, how to focus, humility, ego, and a whole bunch of other things.

"It was quite a lesson. By showing me how useless my ego was when confronted by a superior martial artist, a superior strategist, he was offering me a chance to demonstrate humility before my students and to show them what the possibilities were. They all thought I was pretty amazing back then. When Sensei came, they didn't even have a frame of reference for what he was doing, it was magic. By offering me up as sacrifice to the gods of ego and humility he was giving me a chance to demonstrate to my students what real leadership is all about. I took his orders. I did what I was told. I licked my wounds quietly in private. I led, from the front and on time. He noticed all this and tested me several other times that weekend, but somehow I was found sufficient. He promoted me to *nidan*."

Curtis "It's hard to imagine that he would put that much thought into something like that."

Linden "Why, because most people don't? Most people put very little thought into what they do. The vast majority of people just move through life and either watch it happen or don't even pay attention beyond what's happening before their nose. Very few actually take control of their environment and guide the forces that control their lives. That requires keen observation, wisdom, strength, consciousness, integrity, personal power, warrior spirit, and a desire to actually live one's life rather than exist. Living our life is the greatest opportunity any individual has for developing a strategy and applying a tactical assault toward the accomplishment of the goal. It is a misfortune that most people feel helpless and so out of control when all they have to do is acquire a warrior spirit and attitude toward life.

"When we are pro-active toward all life's many situations we take responsibility. Got fired? Hmmm, need a new strategy, not oh poor, poor miserable me! Wife unhappy? A warrior doesn't sit and wring his hands; he finds out why and makes a decision. Keep her or let her go! If you decide to keep her, find out what she wants!"

Curtis "Now there's a question..."

Linden "You see what I mean. Life is to be lived. I don't mean that we need a list of fifty things we wish to accomplish over the next five years. I mean that we need to know where and in what direction we are going, how far away it is and how to get there. Then the real journey begins and if we are aware we spend our time in wonder and awe at the world around us. Remember that the top of the mountain is the goal but that all life is found on the sides of the mountain, not the top. The sides, the slopes and valleys and paths are where life is found, not on the stone and snow swept vistas of the highest ridge. We walk along, going in our pre-determined direction, mindful of dangers, aware of the beauty and mystery and majesty that surrounds us. We move with purpose, intent on our goals, but always aware of the life that pounds in our veins and the chance of death around the corner. We live in the here and now, never forgetting that if you only live for some future, unreachable goal you will be forever distancing yourself from the beauty of the moment.

"To be a man of power and knowledge, a warrior, is the highest goal we can serve and the lifelong strategy we embrace in Aikido is both ethically and morally consistent with the finest standards of human existence. We embrace the non-attachment of the Buddhist. We love our brother as our self, the way of Jesus. We seek the divine. We do not forget the world around us. Curtis, Arne, you are still on the brink of discovery. Train with all your faculties. Do not fear. Embrace life and death will slip away and only return when your days are complete.

"Remember the Viking credo. Your days are numbered the instant of your birth. You can fear and run away from battle, but you won't live a moment longer. Therefore, cast away fear, live each moment as a warrior and die when your time is due.

"I believe that is our hotel up ahead. Thank you, my friends."

The Dialogs

Afterword

As a final thought I would hope that anyone who has gotten this far would understand that I am sincere when I say that everything in this book might be wrong. I really don't think so, but I make mistakes and am often wrong about things. This does not in any way diminish the truths that I believe to be here between these covers. It only mitigates the idea that I have done anything significant for those who would find this truly annoying.

Humility is a bitch goddess that you must serve constantly if you ever have any hope of realizing a state of true grace. She doesn't like to be lied to, and she knows all about false and fake and insincere. This is why I believe that that the Ninth Pillar of Mastership is humility, but that the nature of the martial artist – one who must believe in his own invincibility – makes attainment nearly impossible. I do believe, however, that if you just focus on the mystery and awesome beauty of what it is that we do, it really shouldn't be too hard to feel truly humble.

When I listen to music played by someone who is a true master of his instrument, I am comforted. When I see a potter throw fifty pounds of clay into something useful and beautiful, I am relieved and proud and humbled all at the same time. When I see a luthier turn rough wood planks into mandolins, guitars and violins I know what true mastery is all about. When I see an *aikidoka* move gracefully and competently it gives me hope for all mankind. Practice harder.

I have actually known individuals who lived their lives as warriors in thought, word and deed. They encountered all the heartbreak and drama endemic to every mortal life and though encumbered by burden and sorrow, fought their way through it all and lived happily ever after.

The end.

Glossary

Aiki The blending of energy.

Aikido Aikido is made up of three Japanese characters: ai - harmony, ki - spirit, mind, or universal energy, do - the way. Thus aikido is the way of harmony with universal energy, or the way of harmonious spirit.

Aikidoka A practitioner of aikido.

Aiki juitsu The ancient art of battling armed samurai empty handed. This art evolved into a practice where both partners fight empty handed. The first art learned by O'Sensei. From this comes the modified techniques we train today and call Aikido.

Aikikai "Aiki association." A term used to designate the organization created by the founder for the dissemination of aikido.

Atemi Striking the body. Strike directed at the attacker for purposes of unbalancing or distraction.

Bokken a wooden practice sword.

Budo Martial way.

Bushido The code of the samurai warriors.

Chinkan Kishin A breathing technique.

Dan Black belt rank.

Do The way of... as in judo, the gentle way.

Dojo cho The head the dojo. Often refers to the business manager.

Dojo The place where we practice aikido.

Doshu Hereditary title for the head of an organization.

Godan 5th degree black belt.

Gi *(do gi)* Training costume consisting of loose trousers and a jacket tied with a long cotton belt.

Hakama The long, flowing trousers worn in traditional Japanese society.

Hai Japanese for yes.

Hanmi Triangular stance. ***Ai Hanmi*** is harmonious stance and ***gyaku hanmi*** is opposite stance.

Hombu dojo A term used to refer to the central dojo of an organization. Thus this usually designates Aikido World Headquarters.

Ikkyo The first wrist pinning technique.

Ikkyu 1st rank below black belt rank (dan rank).

Irimi Entering movement.

Iriminage A throw that uses an entering motion and continues with a large pinwheel like movement. It is designed to kill.

Juji nage Killing technique that throws an opponent onto the unsupported head from waist height.

Kata Martial art form.

Katatedori An attack in which Uke grabs one of Nage's hands in one of his hands.

Katadori An attack in which Uke grabs at Uke's shoulder or lapel.

Katana Two handed killing sword used by Samurai.

Ki Mind, spirit, energy, or vital force.

Kohai A student junior to oneself.

Kokyu Breath. Part of aikido is the development of breath power.

Kokyudosa Training technique done on knees to develop ki.

Kokyuho A method of coordinating breath and body movement.

Kokyunage Breath throw.

Kotegaeshi An outer wrist throw.

Kotodama A practice of intoning various sounds and phonetic components of the Japanese language.

Kung Fu Being of master level proficiency in martial matters. Also a style of fighting.

Kyu White belt rank or any rank below shodan.

Ma Ai Proper distancing or timing with respect to one's partner.

Marubashi The Japanese idea of patience, a sword held over a man's head, is a mirror of this notion that now is now and dead is dead. Therefore we see two men walking toward each other and only enough room for one to pass. Each man can strike only once.

Mokoto no Kokyu Breathing techniques.

Munetsuki A strike to the lower mid section of the stomach.

Nage The person performing the technique.

Nidan 2nd degree black belt.

Nikkyo The second wrist pinning technique.

Nikyu Second rank below black belt rank (dan rank).

O'Sensei Literally, Great Teacher, Morihei Ueshiba, the founder of Aikido.

Randori The practice of warding off multiple attackers in training.

Ryote Mochi Two hands attacking one wrist.

Sabaki Movement.

Samurai Ancient Japanese knights.

Sandan Third degree black belt.

Satori Instantaneous understanding, enlightenment.

Seiza Sitting on one's knees.

Sempai A student senior to oneself.

Sensei Teacher. It is usually considered proper to address the instructor during practice as "Sensei" rather than by his/her name. If the instructor is a permanent instructor for one's dojo or for an organization, it is proper to address him/her as "Sensei" off the mat as well.

Shihan A formal title meaning, approximately, master instructor. A teacher of teachers.

Shinai Split bamboo practice sword.

Shodan First degree black belt.

Shomenuchi A strike to the top of the head.

Suwari Sitting.

Tai Body.

Tai Chi A martial art practiced in ultra slow motion, with no opponent.

Take Musu Aiki A concept of universal oneness.

Tanden A turning movement.

Tenkan Turning movement, turning the body 180 degrees.

Uke Person being thrown (receiving the technique).

Ukemi The art of falling in response to a technique.

Ushiro Backwards or behind.

Waza Techniques.

Yokomen Referring to the side of the head.

Yondan Fourth degree black belt.

Yudansha Those individuals of black belt rank.

Printed in Great Britain
by Amazon.co.uk, Ltd.,
Marston Gate.